ADMETUS

Emma Lazarus

LITERATURE HOUSE / GREGG PRESS
Upper Saddle River, N. J.

Republished in 1970 by
LITERATURE HOUSE
an imprint of The Gregg Press
121 Pleasant Avenue
Upper Saddle River, N. J. 07458

Standard Book Number—8398-1152-7
Library of Congress Card—77-104508

Printed in United States of America

ADMETUS

AND OTHER POEMS.

BY

EMMA LAZARUS.

NEW YORK:
PUBLISHED BY HURD AND HOUGHTON.
Cambridge: Riverside Press.
1871.

Entered according to Act of Congress, in the year 1871, by
EMMA LAZARUS,
in the Office of the Librarian of Congress, at Washington.

RIVERSIDE, CAMBRIDGE:
PRINTED BY H. O. HOUGHTON AND COMPANY.

CONTENTS.

	PAGE
ADMETUS	1
ORPHEUS	25
LOHENGRIN	61
TANNHÄUSER	83

MISCELLANEOUS.

EPOCHS.
- I. Youth 137
- II. Regret 138
- III. Longing 139
- IV. Storm 140
- V. Surprise 141
- VI. Grief 142
- VII. Acceptance 143
- VIII. Loneliness 144
- IX. Sympathy 145
- X. Patience 146
- XI. Hope 147
- XII. Compensation 148
- XIII. Faith 149
- XIV. Work 150
- XV. Victory 151
- XVI. Peace 152

FLORENCE NIGHTINGALE 153
DREAMS 155
ON A TUFT OF GRASS 157
IN THE JEWISH SYNAGOGUE AT NEWPORT . . . 160

CONTENTS.

	PAGE
WINGS	163
IN A SWEDISH GRAVEYARD	165
MARJORIE'S WOOING	168
THE GARDEN OF ADONIS	171
MORNING	174
IN MEMORIAM	176
REALITY	179
HEROES	182
EXULTATION	186
SONNET	188
IDYL	189
THE DAY OF DEAD SOLDIERS	191
HOW LONG	193

TRANSLATIONS.

FRAGMENT FROM THE ITALIAN OF GIACOMO LEOPARDI	197
DEDICATION OF GOETHE'S "FAUST"	199
PROLOGUE FOR THE THEATRE	201
SCENE FROM "FAUST"	210
SONG FROM HEINE	230

ADMETUS.

TO MY FRIEND, RALPH WALDO EMERSON.

ADMETUS.

HE who could beard the lion in his lair,
  To bind him for a girl, and tame the boar,
  And drive these beasts before his chariot,
Might wed Alcestis. For her low brows' sake,
Her hair's soft undulations of warm gold,
Her eyes' clear color and pure virgin mouth,
Though many would draw bow or shiver spear,
Yet none dared meet the intolerable eye,
Or lipless tusk, of lion or of boar.
This heard Admetus, King of Thessaly,
Whose broad, fat pastures spread their ample
    fields
Down to the sheer edge of Amphrysus' stream,
Who laughed, disdainful, at the father's pride,
That set such value on one milk-faced child.

One morning, as he rode alone and passed
Through the green twilight of Thessalian woods,
Between two pendulous branches interlocked,
As through an open casement, he descried

A goddess, as he deemed, — in truth a maid.
On a low bank she fondled tenderly
A favorite hound, her floral face inclined
Above the glossy, graceful animal,
That pressed his snout against her cheek and
    gazed
Wistfully, with his keen, sagacious eyes.
One arm with lax embrace the neck enwreathed,
With polished roundness near the sleek, gray skin.
Admetus, fixed with wonder, dared not pass,
Intrusive on her holy innocence
And sacred girlhood, but his fretful steed
Snuffed the large air, and champed and pawed the
    ground;
And hearing this, the maiden raised her head.
No let or hindrance then might stop the king,
Once having looked upon those supreme eyes.
The drooping boughs disparting, forth he sped,
And then drew in his steed, to ask the path,
Like a lost traveller in an alien land.
Although each river-cloven vale, with streams
Arrowy glancing to the blue Ægean,
Each hallowed mountain, the abode of gods,
Pelion and Ossa fringed with haunted groves,
The height, spring-crowned, of dedicate Olympus,
And pleasant sun-fed vineyards, were to him
Familiar as his own face in the stream,

Nathless he paused and asked the maid what path
Might lead him from the forest. She replied,
But still he tarried, and with sportsman's praise
Admired the hound and stooped to stroke its
　　head,
And asked her if she hunted. Nay, not she:
Her father Pelias hunted in these woods,
Where there was royal game. He knew her now, —
Alcestis, — and he left her with due thanks:
No goddess, but a mortal, to be won
By such a simple feat as driving boars
And lions to his chariot. What was that
To him who saw the boar of Calydon,
The sacred boar of Artemis, at bay
In the broad stagnant marsh, and sent his darts
In its tough, quivering flank, and saw its death,
Stung by sure arrows of Arcadian nymph?

　　To river-pastures of his flocks and herds
Admetus rode, where sweet-breathed cattle grazed,
Heifers and goats and kids, and foolish sheep
Dotted cool, spacious meadows with bent heads,
And necks' soft wool broken in yellow flakes,
Nibbling sharp-toothed the rich, thick-growing blades.
One herdsman kept the innumerable droves —
A boy yet, young as immortality —
In listless posture on a vine-grown rock.

Around him huddled kids and sheep that left
The mother's udder for his nighest grass,
Which sprouted with fresh verdure where he sat.
And yet dull neighboring rustics never guessed
A god had been among them till he went,
Although with him they acted as he willed,
Renouncing shepherds' silly pranks and quips,
Because his very presence made them grave.
Amphryssius, after their translucent stream,
They called him, but Admetus knew his name, —
Hyperion, god of sun and song and silver speech,
Condemned to serve a mortal for his sin
To Zeus in sending violent darts of death,
And raising hand irreverent, against
The one-eyed forgers of the thunderbolt.
For shepherd's crook he held the living rod
Of twisted serpents, later Hermes' wand.
Him sought the king, discovering soon hard by,
Idle, as one in nowise bound to time,
Watching the restless grasses blow and wave,
The sparkle of the sun upon the stream,
Regretting nothing, living with the hour:
For him, who had his light and song within,
Was naught that did not shine, and all things sang.
Admetus prayed for his celestial aid
To win Alcestis, which the god vouchsafed,
Granting with smiles, as grant all gods, who smite

With stern hand, sparing not for piteousness,
But give their gifts in gladness.
                           Thus the king
Led with loose rein the beasts as tame as kine,
And townsfolk thronged within the city streets,
As round a god; and mothers showed their babes,
And maidens loved the crowned intrepid youth,
And men would worship, though the very god
Who wrought the wonder dwelled unnoted nigh,
Divinely scornful of neglect or praise.
Then Pelias, seeing this would be his son,
As he had vowed, called for his wife and child.
With Anaxibia, Alcestis came,
A warm flush spreading o'er her eager face
In looking on the rider of the woods,
And knowing him her suitor and the king.

Admetus won Alcestis thus to wife,
And these with mated hearts and mutual love
Lived a life blameless, beautiful: the king
Ordaining justice in the gates; the queen,
With grateful offerings to the household gods,
Wise with the wisdom of the pure in heart.
One child she bore, — Eumelus, — and he throve.
Yet none the less because they sacrificed
The firstlings of their flocks and fruits and flowers,
Did trouble come; for sickness seized the king.

Alcestis watched with many-handed love,
But unavailing service, for he lay
With languid limbs, despite his ancient strength
Of sinew, and his skill with spear and sword.
His mother came, Clymene, and with her
His father, Pheres: his unconscious child
They brought him, while forlorn Alcestis sat
Discouraged, with the face of desolation.
The jealous gods would bind his mouth from speech,
And smite his vigorous frame with impotence;
And ruin with bitter ashes, worms, and dust,
The beauty of his crowned, exalted head.
He knew her presence, — soon he would not know,
Nor feel her hand in his lie warm and close,
Nor care if she were near him any more.
Exhausted with long vigils, thus the queen
Held hard and grievous thoughts, till heavy sleep
Possessed her weary senses, and she dreamed.
And even in her dream her trouble lived,
For she was praying in a barren field
To all the gods for help, when came across
The waste of air and land, from distant skies,
A spiritual voice divinely clear,
Whose unimaginable sweetness thrilled
Her aching heart with tremor of strange joy:
"Arise, Alcestis, cast away white fear.

A god dwells with you : seek, and you shall find."
Then quiet satisfaction filled her soul
Almost akin to gladness, and she woke.
Weak as the dead, Admetus lay there still;
But she, superb with confidence, arose,
And passed beyond the mourners' curious eyes,
Seeking Amphryssius in the meadow-lands.
She found him with the godlike mien of one
Who, roused, awakens unto deeds divine :
" I come, Hyperion, with incessant tears,
To crave the life of my dear lord the king.
Pity me, for I see the future years
Widowed and laden with disastrous days.
And ye, the gods, will miss him when the fires
Upon your shrines, unfed, neglected die.
Who will pour large libations in your names,
And sacrifice with generous piety ?
Silence and apathy will greet you there
Where once a splendid spirit offered praise.
Grant me this boon divine, and I will beat
With prayer at morning's gates, before they ope
Unto thy silver-hoofed and flame-eyed steeds.
Answer ere yet the irremeable stream
Be crossed : answer, O god, and save ! "
           She ceased,
With full throat salt with tears, and looked on him,
And with a sudden cry of awe fell prone,

For, lo! he was transmuted to a god;
The supreme aureole radiant round his brow,
Divine refulgence on his face, — his eyes
Awful with splendor, and his august head
With blinding brilliance crowned by vivid flame.
Then in a voice that charmed the listening air:
"Woman, arise! I have no influence
On Death, who is the servant of the Fates.
Howbeit for thy passion and thy prayer,
The grace of thy fair womanhood and youth,
Thus godlike will I intercede for thee,
And sue the insatiate sisters for this life.
Yet hope not blindly: loth are these to change
Their purpose; neither will they freely give,
But haggling lend or sell: perchance the price
Will countervail the boon. Consider this.
Now rise and look upon me." And she rose,
But by her stood no godhead bathed in light,
But young Amphryssius, herdsman to the king,
Benignly smiling.   Fleet as thought, the god
Fled from the glittering earth to blackest depths
Of Tartarus; and none might say he sped
On wings ambrosial, or with feet as swift
As scouring hail, or airy chariot
Borne by flame-breathing steeds ethereal;
But with a motion inconceivable

Departed and was there. Before the throne
Of Ades, first he hailed the long-sought queen,
Stolen with violent hands from grassy fields
And delicate airs of sunlit Sicily,
Pensive, gold-haired, but innocent-eyed no more
As when she laughing plucked the daffodils,
But grave as one fulfilling a strange doom.
And low at Ades' feet, wrapped in grim murk
And darkness thick, the three gray women sat,
Loose-robed and chapleted with wool and flowers,
Purple narcissi round their horrid hair.
Intent upon her task, the first one held
The slender thread that at a touch would snap;
The second weaving it with warp and woof
Into strange textures, some stained dark and foul,
Some sanguine-colored, and some black as night,
And rare ones white, or with a golden thread
Running throughout the web: the farthest hag
With glistening scissors cut her sisters' work.
To these Hyperion, but they never ceased,
Nor raised their eyes, till with soft, moderate tones,
But by their powerful persuasiveness
Commanding all to listen and obey,
He spoke, and all hell heard, and these three looked
And waited his request:

     "I come, a god,
At a pure mortal queen's request, who sues

For life renewed unto her dying lord,
Admetus; and I also pray this prayer."
"Then cease, for when hath Fate been moved by
　prayer?"
"But strength and upright heart should serve with
　you."
"Nay, these may serve with all but Destiny."
"I ask ye not forever to forbear,
But spare a while, — a moment unto us,
A lifetime unto men." "The Fates swerve not
For supplications, like the pliant gods.
Have they not willed a life's thread should be cut?
With them the will is changeless as the deed.
O men! ye have not learned in all the past
Desires are barren and tears yield no fruit.
How long will ye besiege the thrones of gods
With lamentations? When lagged Death for all
Your timorous shirking? We work not like you,
Delaying and relenting, purposeless,
With unenduring issues; but our deeds,
Forever interchained and interlocked,
Complete each other and explain themselves."
"Ye will a life: then why not any life?"
"What care we for the king? He is not worth
These many words: indeed, we love not speech.
We care not if he live, or lose such life
As men are greedy for, — filled full with hate,

ADMETUS.

Sins beneath scorn, and only lit by dreams,
Or one sane moment, or a useless hope, —
Lasting how long ? — the space between the green
And fading yellow of the grass they tread."
But he withdrawing not: "Will any life
Suffice ye for Admetus?" "Yea," the crones
Three times repeated. "We know no such names
As king or queen or slaves: we want but life.
Begone, and vex us in our work no ₁more."

With broken blessings, inarticulate joy
And tears, Alcestis thanked Hyperion,
And worshipped. Then he gently: "Who will die,
So that the king may live?" And she: "You ask?
Nay, who will live when life clasps hands with shame,
And death with honor? Lo, you are a god;
You cannot know the highest joy of life, —
To leave it when 'tis worthier to die.
His parents, kinsmen, courtiers, subjects, slaves, —
For love of him myself would die, were none
Found ready; but what Greek would stand to see
A woman glorified, and falter? Once,
And only once, the gods will do this thing
In all the ages: such a man themselves
Delight to honor, — holy, temperate, chaste,
With reverence for his dæmon and his god."
Thus she triumphant to the very door

Of King Admetus' chamber. All there saw
Her ill-timed gladness with much wonderment.
But she: "No longer mourn! The king is saved:
The Fates will spare him. Lift your voice in praise;
Sing pæans to Apollo; crown your brows
With laurel; offer thankful sacrifice!"
"O Queen, what mean these foolish words misplaced?
And what an hour is this to thank the Fates?"
"Thrice blessed be the gods! — for God himself
Has sued for me, — they are not stern and deaf.
Cry, and they answer: commune with your soul,
And they send counsel: weep with rainy grief,
And these will sweeten you your bitterest tears.
On one condition King Admetus lives,
And ye, on hearing, will lament no more,
Each emulous to save." Then — for she spake
Assured, as having heard an oracle —
They asked: "What deed of ours may serve the king?"
"The Fates accept another life for his,
And one of you may die." Smiling, she ceased.
But silence answered her. "What! do ye thrust
Your arrows in your hearts beneath your cloaks,
Dying like Greeks, too proud to own the pang?
This ask I not. In all the populous land
But one need suffer for immortal praise.

The generous Fates have sent no pestilence,
Famine, nor war: it is as though they gave
Freely, and only make the boon more rich
By such slight payment. Now a people mourns,
And ye may change the grief to jubilee,
Filling the cities with a pleasant sound.
But as for me, what faltering words can tell
My joy, in extreme sharpness kin to pain?
A monument you have within my heart,
Wreathed with kind love and dear remembrances;
And I will pray for you before I crave
Pardon and pity for myself from God.
Your name will be the highest in the land,
Oftenest, fondest on my grateful lips,
After the name of him you die to save.
What! silent still? Since when has virtue grown
Less beautiful than indolence and ease?
Is death more terrible, more hateworthy,
More bitter than dishonor? Will ye live
On shame? Chew and find sweet its poisoned
  fruits?
What sons will ye bring forth — mean-souled like
  you,
Or, like your parents, brave — to blush like girls,
And say, 'Our fathers were afraid to die!'
Ye will not dare to raise heroic eyes
Unto the eyes of aliens. In the streets

Will women and young children point at you
Scornfully, and the sun will find you shamed,
And night refuse to shield you. What a life
Is this ye spin and fashion for yourselves!
And what new tortures of suspense and doubt
Will death invent for such as are afraid!
Acastus, thou my brother, in the field
Foremost, who greeted me with sanguine hands
From ruddy battle with a conqueror's face, —
These honors wilt thou blot with infamy?
Nay, thou hast won no honors: a mere girl
Would do as much as thou at such a time,
In clamorous battle, 'midst tumultuous sounds,
Neighing of war-steeds, shouts of sharp command,
Snapping of shivered spears; for all are brave
When all men look to them expectantly;
But he is truly brave who faces death
Within his chamber, at a sudden call,
At night, when no man sees, — content to die
When life can serve no longer those he loves."
Then thus Acastus: "Sister, I fear not
Death, nor the empty darkness of the grave,
And hold my life but as a little thing,
Subject unto my people's call, and Fate.
But if 'tis little, no greater is the king's;
And though my heart bleeds sorely, I recall
Astydamia, who thus would mourn for me.

We are not cowards, we youth of Thessaly,
And Thessaly — yea, all Greece — knoweth it;
Nor will we brook the name from even you,
Albeit a queen, and uttering these wild words
Through your unwonted sorrow." Then she knew
That he stood firm, and turning from him, cried
To the king's parents: " Are ye deaf with grief,
Pheres, Clymene? Ye can save your son,
Yet rather stand and weep with barren tears.
O, shame! to think that such gray, reverend hairs
Should cover such unvenerable heads!
What would ye lose? — a remnant of mere life,
A few slight raveled threads, and give him years
To fill with glory. Who, when he is gone,
Will call you gentlest names this side of heaven, —
Father and mother? Knew ye not this man
Ere he was royal, — a poor, helpless child,
Crownless and kingdomless? One birth alone
Sufficeth not, Clymene: once again
You must give life with travail and strong pain.
Has he not lived to outstrip your swift hopes?
What mother can refuse a second birth
To such a son? But ye denying him,
What after offering may appease the gods?
What joy outweigh the grief of this one day?
What clamor drown the hours' myriad tongues,
Crying, 'Your son, your son? where is your son,

Unnatural mother, timid, foolish man?"
Then Pheres gravely: "These are graceless words
From you our daughter. Life is always life,
And death comes soon enough to such as we.
We twain are old and weak, have served our time,
And made our sacrifices. Let the young
Arise now in their turn and save the king."
"O gods! look on your creatures! do ye see?
And seeing, have ye patience? Smite them all,
Unsparing, with dishonorable death.
Vile slaves! a woman teaches you to die.
Intrepid, with exalted steadfast soul,
Scorn in my heart, and love unutterable,
I yield the Fates my life, and like a god
Command them to revere that sacred head.
Thus kiss I thrice the dear, blind, holy eyes,
And bid them see; and thrice I kiss this brow,
And thus unfasten I the pale, proud lips
With fruitful kissings, bringing love and life,
And without fear or any pang, I breathe
My soul in him."
    "Alcestis, I awake.
I hear, I hear — unspeak thy reckless words!
For, lo! thy life-blood tingles in my veins,
And streameth through my body like new wine.
Behold! thy spirit dedicate revives
My pulse, and through thy sacrifice I breathe.

ADMETUS.

Thy lips are bloodless: kiss me not again.
Ashen thy cheeks, faded thy flower-like hands.
O woman! perfect in thy womanhood
And in thy wifehood, I adjure thee now
As mother, by the love thou bearest our child,
In this thy hour of passion and of love,
Of sacrifice and sorrow, to unsay
Thy words sublime!" "I die that thou mayest live."
" And deemest thou that I accept the boon,
Craven, like these my subjects? Lo, my queen,
Is life itself a lovely thing, — bare life?
And empty breath a thing desirable?
Or is it rather happiness and love
That make it precious to its inmost core?
When these are lost, are there not swords in Greece,
And flame and poison, deadly waves and plagues?
No man has ever lacked these things and gone
Unsatisfied. It is not these the gods refuse
(Nay, never clutch my sleeve and raise thy lip), —
Not these I seek; but I will stab myself,
Poison my life and burn my flesh, with words,
And save or follow thee. Lo! hearken now:
I bid the gods take back their loathsome gifts:
I spurn them, and I scorn them, and I hate.
Will they prove deaf to this as to my prayers?
With tongue reviling, blasphemous, I curse,

With mouth polluted from deliberate heart.
Dishonored be their names, scorned be their priests,
Ruined their altars, mocked their oracles!
It is Admetus, King of Thessaly,
Defaming thus: annihilate him, gods!
So that his queen, who worships you, may live."
He paused as one expectant; but no bolt
From the insulted heavens answered him,
But awful silence followed. Then a hand,
A boyish hand, upon his shoulder fell,
And turning, he beheld his shepherd boy,
Not wrathful, but divinely pitiful,
Who spake in tender, thrilling tones: "The gods
Cannot recall their gifts. Blaspheme them not:
Bow down and worship rather. Shall he curse
Who sees not, and who hears not, — neither knows
Nor understands? Nay, thou shalt bless and pray, —
Pray, for the pure heart, purged by prayer, divines
And seeth when the bolder eyes are blind.
Worship and wonder, — these befit a man
At every hour; and mayhap will the gods
Yet work a miracle for knees that bend
And hands that supplicate."
                        Then all they knew
A sudden sense of awe, and bowed their heads
Beneath the stripling's gaze: Admetus fell,

Crushed by that gentle touch, and cried aloud:
" Pardon and pity! I am hard beset."

    There waited at the doorway of the king
One grim and ghastly, shadowy, horrible,
Bearing the likeness of a king himself,
Erect as one who serveth not, — upon
His head a crown, within his fleshless hands
A sceptre, — monstrous, winged, intolerable.
To him a stranger coming 'neath the trees,
Which slid down flakes of light, now on his hair,
Close-curled, now on his bared and brawny chest,
Now on his flexile, vine-like veinéd limbs,
With iron network of strong muscle thewed,
And godlike brows and proud mouth unrelaxed.
Firm was his step; no superfluity
Of indolent flesh impeded this man's strength.
Slender and supple every perfect limb,
Beautiful with the glory of a man.
No weapons bare he, neither shield: his hands
Folded upon his breast, his movements free
Of all incumbrance. When his mighty strides
Had brought him nigh the waiting one, he paused:
" Whose palace this? and who art thou, grim shade?"
" The palace of the King of Thessaly,

And my name is not strange unto thine ears;
For who hath told men that I wait for them,
The one sure thing on earth? Yet all they know,
Unasking and yet answered. I am Death,
The only secret that the gods reveal.
But who art thou who darest question me?"
"Alcides; and that thing I dare not do
Hath found no name. Whom here awaitest thou?"
"Alcestis, Queen of Thessaly, — a queen
Who wooed me as the bridegroom woos the bride,
For her life sacrificed will save her lord
Admetus, as the Fates decreed. I wait
Impatient, eager; and I enter soon,
With darkening wing, invisible, a god,
And kiss her lips, and kiss her throbbing heart,
And then the tenderest hands can do no more
Than close her eyes and wipe her cold, white brow,
Inurn her ashes and strew flowers above."
"This woman is a god, a hero, Death.
In this her sacrifice I see a soul
Luminous, starry: earth can spare her not:
It is not rich enough in purity
To lose this paragon. Save her, O Death!
Thou surely art more gentle than the Fates,
Yet these have spared her lord, and never meant
That she should suffer, and that this their grace,
Beautiful, royal on one side, should turn

Sudden and show a fearful, fatal face."
"Nay, have they not? O fond and foolish man,
Naught comes unlooked for, unforeseen by them.
Doubt when they favor thee, though thou mayest laugh
When they have scourged thee with an iron scourge.
Behold, their smile is deadlier than their sting,
And every boon of theirs is double-faced.
Yea, I am gentler unto ye than these:
I slay relentless, but when have I mocked
With poisoned gifts, and generous hands that smite
Under the flowers? for my name is Truth.
Were this fair queen more fair, more pure, more chaste,
I would not spare her for your wildest prayer
Nor her best virtue. Is the earth's mouth full?
Is the grave satisfied? Discrown me then,
For life is lord, and men may mock the gods
With immortality." "I sue no more,
But I command thee spare this woman's life,
Or wrestle with Alcides." "Wrestle with thee,
Thou puny boy!" And Death laughed loud, and swelled
To monstrous bulk, fierce-eyed, with outstretched wings,

And lightnings round his brow; but grave and
    firm,
Strong as a tower, Alcides waited him,
And these began to wrestle, and a cloud
Impenetrable fell, and all was dark.

"Farewell, Admetus and my little son,
Eumelus, — O these clinging baby hands!
Thy loss is bitter, for no chance, no fame,
No wealth of love, can ever compensate
For a dead mother. Thou, O king, fulfill
The double duty: love him with my love,
And make him bold to wrestle, shiver spears,
Noble and manly, Grecian to the bone;
And tell him that his mother spake with gods.
Farewell, farewell! Mine eyes are growing blind:
The darkness gathers. O my heart, my heart!"
No sound made answer save the cries of grief
From all the mourners, and the suppliance
Of strick'n Admetus: "O have mercy, gods!
O gods, have mercy, mercy upon us!"
Then from the dying woman's couch again
Her voice was heard, but with strange sudden tones:
"Lo, I awake, — the light comes back to me.
What miracle is this?" And thunders shook

The air, and clouds of mighty darkness fell,
And the earth trembled, and weird, horrid sounds
Were heard of rushing wings and fleeing feet,
And groans; and all were silent, dumb with awe,
Saving the king, who paused not in his prayer:
" Have mercy, gods ! " and then again, " O gods,
Have mercy ! "
    Through the open casement poured
Bright floods of sunny light; the air was soft,
Clear, delicate as though a summer storm
Had passed away ; and those there standing saw,
Afar upon the plain, Death fleeing thence,
And at the doorway, weary, well-nigh spent,
Alcides, flushed with victory.

ORPHEUS.

TO MY SISTER JOSEPHINE.

1869.

ORPHEUS.

ORPHEUS.

LAUGHTER and dance, and sounds of harp
    and lyre,
  Piping of flutes, singing of festal songs,
Ribbons of flame from flaunting torches, dulled
By the broad summer sunshine, these had filled
Since the high noon the pillared vestibules,
The peristyles and porches, in the house
Of the bride's father. Maidens, garlanded
With rose and myrtle dedicate to Love,
Adorned with chaplets fresh the bride, and veiled
The shining head and wistful, girlish face,
Ineffable sweetness of divided lips,
Large light of clear, gray eyes, low, lucid brows,
White as a cloud, beneath pale, clustering gold.
When sunless skies uncertain twilight cast,
That makes a friend's face as an alien's strange,
Investing with a foreign mystery
The dear green fields about our very home.

Then waiting stood the gilded chariot
Before the porch, and from the vine-wreathed door,
Issued the white-veiled bride, while jocund youths
And mænads followed her with dance and song.
She came with double glory; for her lord,
Son of Apollo and Calliope,
Towered beside her, beautiful in limb
And feature, as though formed to magic strains,
Like the Bœotian city, that arose
In airy structures to Amphion's lute.
The light serene shone from his brow and eyes,
Of one whose lofty thoughts keep consonance
With the celestial music of the spheres.
His smile was fluent, and his speech outsang
The cadences of soft-stringed instruments.

 He to the chariot led Eurydice,
And these twain, mounting with their paranymph,
Drove onward through the dusky twilit fields,
Preceded by the nymphs and singing youths,
And boys diffusing light and odors warm,
With flaming brands of aromatic woods,
And matrons bearing symbols of the life
Of careful wives, the distaff and the sieve;
And followed by the echoes of their songs,
The fragrance crushed from moist and trodden grass,
The blessing of the ever-present gods,

Whom they invoked with earnest hymns and
  prayer.
From Orpheus' portico, festooned with vines,
Issued a flood of rare, ambrosial light,
As though Olympian portals stood ajar,
And Hymen, radiant by his torch's flame,
Mystic with saffron vest and purple, stood
With hands munificent to greet and bless.
Ripe fruits were poured upon the married pair
Alighting, and the chariot wheels were burnt,
A token that the bride returned no more
Unto her father's house. With step resolved,
She crossed the threshold soft with flowers, secure
That his heroic soul who guided her,
Was potent and alert to grace her life,
With noble outlines and ideal hues,
Uplifting it to equal height with his.

EPITHALAMIUM. TO ZEUS.

Because thou art enthroned beyond our reach,
Behind the brightest and the farthest star,
And silence is as eloquent as speech,
To thee who knowest us for what we are,
We bring thee naught save brief and simple prayer,
Strong in its naked, frank sincerity.
Send sacred joys of marriage to this pair,
With fertile increase and prosperity.

Three nymphs had met beneath an oak that cast
Cool, dappled shadow on the glowing grass,
And liquid gleam of the translucent brook.
The air was musical with frolic sounds
Of feminine voices, and of laughter blithe.
Patines of sunshine fell like mottled gold
On the rose-white of bright bare limbs and neck,
On flowing, snowy mantles, and again
With sudden splendor on the gloriole
Of warm, rich hair. The fairest nymph reclined
Beneath the tree, and leaned her yellow head,
With its crisp, clustering rings, against the trunk,
And dipped her pure feet in the colorless brook,
Stirring the ripples into circles wide,
With cool, delicious plashings in the stream.
Her young companions lay upon the grass,
With indolent eyes half closed, and parted lips
Half-smiling, in the languor of the noon.
But suddenly these twain, arising, cried,
Startled and sharply, " Lo, Eurydice,
Behold ! " and she, uplifting frightened eyes,
Saw a strange shepherd watching with bold glance.
Veiling their faces with their mantles light,
Her sisters fled swift-footed, with shrill cries,
Adown the meadow, but her wet feet clung
To the dry grasses and the earthy soil.
" Eurydice, I love thee ! fear me not,

For I am Aristæus, with gray groves
Of hoary olives, and innumerous flocks,
And precious swarms of yellow-vested bees."
But she with sudden strength eluding him,
Sprang o'er the flowery turf, with back-blown hair,
And wing-like garments, shortened breath, and face
Kindled with shame and terror. In her flight
She ran through fatal flowers and tangled weeds;
And thick rank grass beside a stagnant pool,
When, with a keen and breathless cry of pain,
Abrupt she fell amidst the tall, green reeds.
Then Aristæus reached her, as a snake
Crept back in sinuous lines amidst the slime.
Desire was changed to pity, when he saw
The wounded dryad in her agony
Strive vainly to escape, repelling him
With feeble arms. " Forgive me, nymph," he cried ;
" I will not touch, save with most reverent hands,
Thy sacred form. But let me bear thee hence,
And soothe thy bruise with healing herbs. " Too late,
Leave me," she sighed, "and lead thou Orpheus here,
That I may see him ere the daylight fails."
He left her pale with suffering, — earth seemed strange
Unto her eyes, who knew she looked her last

On level-stretching meadows, hazy hills,
And all the light and color of the sky.
Brief as a dream she saw her happy life,
Her father's face, her mother's blessed eyes,
The hero who, unheralded, appeared,
And all was changed, — all things put forth a voice,
As in the season of the singing birds.
She looked around revived, and saw again
The lapsing river and abiding sky.
Across the sunny fields came Aristæus,
With Orpheus following, — and after these,
Sad nymphs and heroes grave with sympathy.
Quite calm she lay, and almost wished to die
Before they reached her, if the throbbing pain
Of limb and heart could only thus be stilled.
But Orpheus hastened to her side, and mourned,
"Eurydice, Eurydice! Remain, —
For there is no delight of speech nor song
Among the dead. Will the gods jest with me,
And call this life, which must forevermore
Be but a void, a hunger, a desire,
A stretching out of empty hands to grasp
What earth nor sea nor heaven will restore?
Is this the life that I conceived and sang,
Rich with all noble opportunities
And beautiful realities?" But she:
"Brave Orpheus, search thou not the eternal gods,

Surely they love us dearer than we know.
Do thou refrain, for yet I hold my faith.
When I am gone, thou still wilt have thy lyre;
Love it and cherish, — it is Fate's best gift,
And with death's clearer vision, I can see
That in all ages men will be upraised
Nearer to gods through this than through aught else.
My death may but inspire a larger note,
A passionate cadence to thy strain, which else
Were not quite human, and thus incomplete.
And with this thought I am content to die.
Cease not to sing to me when I am gone;
Thy voice will reach me in the farthest spheres,
Or wake me out of silence. Now begin,
That I may float on those celestial waves
Into the darkness, as I oft have longed."

ORPHEUS.

Once in a wild, bright vision, came to me
  Beautiful music, luminous as morn,
  An effluence of light and rapture born,
With eyes as full of splendor as the sea;
  Dazzling as youth, with pinions frail as air,
  Yet potent to uplift and soar as prayer.
Again I see her, cypress in her wreath,
  Sad with all grave and tender mysteries;

Tears in her unimaginable eyes,
That look their first with wondering awe on Death.

Never again, in all the after years,
  Will her lips laugh with utter mirthfulness;
  Nor the strange longing in her eyes grow less,
Nor any time dispel their mist of tears.
  Yea, with new numbers she completes her strain,
  A song unsung before by gods or men;
But she hath lost, ah! lost for evermore,
  The ringing note of joy ineffable,
  The high assurance proud, that all is well,
The glad refrain that pealed from shore to shore.

O lyre, thou hast done with joyous things,
  Triumphant ecstasies, exultant song;
  Of subtle pain, keen anguish, hopeless wrong,
I fashion now another of thy strings,
  And strike thee with a strong hand passionate,
  Into a fuller music, adequate
Unto a soul that seeks insatiably,
  With fond, illusive hope and faith divine;
  For through all ages will my soul seek thine,
Eurydice, my lost Eurydice!

ORPHEUS.

What solace to lament with empty hands
And smitten heart, above a mound of earth,
Vivid with mockery of perpetual flowers,
O'er one small urn that holds beneath its lid,
With overmeasure, all the flameless dust
And soulless ashes of our love? Yet this
Was Orpheus' life, to mourn beside the grave,
From his stringed lyre compelling wild response,
And thrilling intonation of his grief,
That made the hearts of gnarled and knotty oaks
Ache as with human sympathy, and rived
The adamantine centre of the rock,
And lured the forest beasts, and hushed the birds,
Mavis and lark, while with wide, awful wings,
The eagle shadowed his exalted brow.
" Surely," he cried, " the senseless dust hears not,
More than the burnt brand hears old natural sounds
Innumerable rustle of young leaves.
It cannot be that only these remain,
The ashes of her glittering limbs, warm flesh,
And blessed hair, — my love had more than these
Where is the vital soul, that was to me
An inspiration and an influence?
The gods are not unstable like rash man,
Aimlessly to create and discreate,
With cruel and capricious fantasy,
For thus the immaculate skies would be a lie;

Eurydice is but withdrawn from me,
And disembodied, while mine eyesight blinds,
My senses are a hindrance, and obstruct
The accurate perception of my soul.
When mine own spirit, nightly disenthralled,
Soars to the land of dreams, whose boundaries,
By day,-loom infinitely far and vague,
And yet, at night, become our very home, —
There still I see thee with the same bright form,
The same auroral eyes that made for me
Perpetual morning; and I stretch mine arms
Hungering after thee, and, calling, wake
Unto the vapid glare of languid dawn.
Yet all these things address my very soul,
Telling it that thou art not dead; for death
Is but the incarnation of man's fears;
Gods do not recognize it. If thou art
(As I have faith) in the known universe,
Yea, though it be in the extremest land,
Beyond the sunset, with its shining isles,
I will go forth and seek thee, nor will cease
To mourn thee and desire, till I have found."

    Thus Orpheus fared across the full-fed streams
Of Hebrus and of Strymon, and beyond
The purple outlines and aerial crags,
Snow-glittering of Scardus, Rhodope,

And grand Orbelus; through fair, fertile fields
Of Thessaly with increase of ripe corn,
Through Attica, Bœotia and Eubœa,
And southward to the royal-citied state,
Beautiful Corinth, throned upon the base
Of green Acrocorinthus, whose soft slope
Was dedicate with temples to the gods,
And towering over all the sacred shrine
Of Aphrodite. Upward from the town
The mountain rose defensive, where the walls
Of Corinth ended, and beyond the gates,
The radiant plain of the Corinthian Gulf
Stretched infinitely. Orpheus rested here,
Till he bethought him to ascend the mount,
With offerings at Aphrodite's shrine —
Not sanguine victims, but fresh myrtle wreath
And faultless rose — to sue the oracle
For help and guidance.
                All the town was still,
The bright red band of sunrise lit the sky
Above the dark blue gulf, and Orpheus heard
A hundred birds saluting, from the brake,
Aurora, and cool rush of waterfalls
Made murmurous music, while Athené breathed
The vigor of the morning in his soul.
Up the steep mountain side he passed, beyond
The silver growth of olives, and the belt
Of pines, to where the foam-white temple stood,

Smitten at once by all the beams of morn.
He saw the double peak, rose-white with snow
And early sunshine, of Parnassus cleave
The northern sky, and sacred Helicon
Erect its head, crowned with the Muses' grove.
The Bay of Crissa and Corinthian Gulf,
Below flashed restless, and a path of gold
Divided with clear, tremulous light the waves.
From the large beauty of the morn, he went
Into the holy limits of the shrine,
With warm air heavy with the odorous rose.

ORPHEUS.

I put into my prayer to thee, O mother,
The tumult and the passion of the ocean,
The unflecked purity of winnowed foam-wreaths;

To thee who sprang from these, the incarnation
Of all the huge sea holds of grace or splendor,
With its own light between thine amorous eyelids.

For I, in thy most sacred cause a pilgrim,
Have wandered tireless, from Thrace to Corinth,
'Midst foreign scenes and alien men and women.

And at my right hand Grief incessant follows,
And at my left walks Memory with the semblance
Of lost Eurydice's ethereal beauty.

Infatuate I gaze, until the vision
Thrills me to madness, and I start and tremble,
Remembering also Grief is my companion.

Onward through spacious fields, by copious waters,
Through purple growth of amaranth and crocus,
And past the marble beauty of great cities,

We three have journeyed, — strangers saw me reckless,
And knew at once that I had walked with sorrow,
And that the gods had chosen me their victim.

Are all my carols useless, worse than useless?
Shall my long pilgrimage, thus unrewarded,
End at the blank, insuperable ocean?

Hast thou no wise compassion, goddess, mother?
In all the measureless years' unfathomed chances,
Is the dear past to be repeated never?

O supreme mother! crowned with blessed poppy
As well as myrtle, — bring her here, or compass
My soul with death, that elsewhere I may seek her.

He ceased, and through the temple spread a mist
Ambrosial, and above the shrine a star
Serenely brightened, and a heavenly voice
Made sweet response: " Love guides himself thy
    course
To the last sea-girt rock. No worthy soul
May ever truly seek, and fail to find."

Still southward Orpheus journeyed, till he reached
Cape Tænarus, the last bleak point of Greece,
Desolate o'er an infinite waste of waves,
While sunset lit the western sea and sky
With yellow floods of warm, diffusive light,
Kindling his serious face and earnest eyes,
And glittering on his lyre. Long time he stood,
And gazed upon the trouble of the waves,
Expectant of a word, a sign — and still
No answer made the wild, indifferent sea.
Impetuous, he smote his quivering lyre
To reckless and sonorous melody,
Vibrating o'er the watery turbulence.
Then far below its western bath, the sun
Dipped and was gone, and all the sea was gray.
Still through the air rang those imploring notes,
Unutterably plaintive — till there came
From out the ocean cave of Tænarus
The shining forms of Oceanides,

With myriad faces raised supremely fair,
And myriad arms that beckoned as he sang.
Behold! a stir amidst the frothing brine,
As though upheaved by powers submarine,
In implicate confusion, wave on wave,
Then rose with windy manes and fiery eyes,
Proudly careering, the immortal steeds,
Bearing, within the shell-shaped car, the god
Of august aspect and imperial port,
With such profusion of ambrosial locks
As curl around the very front of Zeus.
He with benign regard the minstrel viewed,
Then whirling thrice his massy trident, struck
The scarpéd promontory with its fork.
And Orpheus felt the solid basis yield,
And heard the hollow rumbling, as when earth
Rocks to her centre, and high hills spit flame.
And lo! he stood before a sulphurous throne,
Set in an open space, wherefrom there streamed
Four rivers stagnant, black. Here Ades reigned,
His very presence unto mortal sense
Oppressive as low thunder in the air.
The triple-headed guardian of his realm
Crouched at his feet, and in the dismal murk,
The hideous Harpies hovered o'er his head.
The serpent-haired Eumenides stood near,
Brow-bound with sanguine fillets, and the Fates

Wielded the distaff, spindle, and sharp shears.
The air was dense with noisome influence,
And shadowy apparitions seemed to float
Athwart the dusk. But on the infernal throne
Conspicuous in beauty, by her lord,
Persephone was seated. Wonderment
Looked from her eyes, in seeing him, no god,
Who came before his time among the dead,
Unarmed with spear or shield, a glistening lyre
Nigh slipping from the loose grasp of his hands.
" Who comes unsummoned to my realm ? " began
The baleful godhead in discordant tones,
Widely reverberant ; and the low, clear voice
Of Orpheus answered : " One who would remain,
If but the impotent body could be free
To follow the desires of the soul, —
Orpheus, an unskilled singer." " Birth and death
Are preordained for thee, presumptuous man.
What narrow space of time the Fates accord,
'Twould best become thee to bear worthily,
With dignity, and leave the rest to them,
The end as the beginning." " Plead for me,
O beautiful Persephone, — behold !
Eurydice was snatched with violent hand
From out mine eager arms, and I have sought
Her image o'er the peopled earth in vain."
Then she : " I may not summon her, nor hope

To swerve the haughty purpose of my lord.
With influence of thy familiar voice,
If thou canst touch her spirit, she is thine."
But Ades: "Who recalls the dead by prayer?
They whose calm souls are once possessed by death,
Find such a solid joy in grasping firm,
After life's phantasms, this reality,
That wisdom, grief, nor love persuadeth them
Their liberated spirits to confine
With fleshly limitations. Nathless sing, —
And prove life's glittering evanescence vain,
Outweighed by death's sublime security."

ORPHEUS.

I render thanks, eternal gods, that ye
Empower myself to call Eurydice.
Man only can fulfill his own desire;
And if I fail, the sorrow rests with me.

Ye give what we deserve; I pray alone
Ne'er to be cursed with what I have not won.
And to whom else would I intrust my lyre,
This supreme invocation to intone?

But in myself I feel the love, the power,
The lyric inspiration, while the flower
Of all my life brings forth its proper fruit,
In this my loftiest, most godlike hour.

If I could make ye feel the agony
Of the strong man, O gods, condemned to see
The light fail from dear eyes, the white lips mute,
The elusive soul take flight eternally

To where we cannot follow it nor find,
With the most subtle searchings of the mind,
With the most passionate longings of the soul,
Deaf, unresponsive as the empty wind;

Then would your pity as your power be,
'Twould crown us all with immortality,
And grace us with completeness, make us whole,
Worthy to be the peers of deity.

For we are mighty now to slay and bless,
Yea, gifted with strange strength of steadfastness,
To conquer bodiless and viewless foes
Within ourselves, yet in our helplessness,

As children, in the presence of this Death,
Whom nor revolt nor patience conquereth,
Implacable, with grim mouth fastened close,
That with no hope our anguish answereth.

Resound with wildest utterance, O my lyre;
Let each note be a living flame of fire,

To reach her, to burn through her, to compel,
Strong with the infinite strength of my desire.

I am no god, yet Fate, Eurydice,
A goddess for my slave hath given me, —
Immortal Music, pure, ineffable;
And I send her, my handmaid, after thee.

If all wherein I put my faith as sure,
Be not delusions vain which death will cure;
If the sublime reliance of the soul
On her own powers be no empty lure,

Whereat the high gods laugh in bitter scorn;
If what I have achieved and what forborne,
Will lead me nearer to a worthy goal,
If all life's promises be not forsworn, —

Eurydice, appear! Before mine eyes,
O gods, I see a formless essence rise,
That moulds itself unto the music's beat,
Appareled in the glory of the skies.

Now, while I ring a more celestial tone,
The spirit more divinely bright hath grown,
To larger modulations, strains complete,
The white limbs from the shapeless mist are won,

As from the bosom of a summer cloud,
Wherewith a goddess would her semblance shroud.
Is this mine own creation? Is it truth,
That with warm life I have blank air endowed?

The soft cloud parts asunder, — yea, 'tis she!
Once more the face that was my star I see,
Crowned with the beauty of immortal youth,
Eurydice, my lost Eurydice!

 Silent beside his silent, fallen lyre,
The singer stood, and clasped her in his arms,
Gazing upon this pale, fair face as one
Whose heart's supreme desire is satisfied.
"Is not this hour the hour I have foreseen,
Through all obstructions and infirmities
Of my mortality, and is it not
More glorious in fruition than I dreamed!
Yea, I have dreamed it all, eternal gods,
Even as now have pressed her to my heart
With the same clinging effort to retain,
And seen this breathing form, these lucent eyes
Vivid as now, instinct with life and love.
Yet have I waked to chill discouragement,
To vacant disappointment, and the sense

Of aching, unassuaged desire. O speak,
For in my dreams I never hear thy voice,
Save veiled and indistinct, a mockery
Of the old limpid music. Speak to me:
Thy flesh is warm, thy heart beats close to mine,
Thine upturned face is wet with human tears;
O speak to me, — lest I should wake again
To barren fields and empty skies of Thrace."
Then in low, natural tones, Eurydice:
" Thy voice hath reached me in the farthest spheres,
And waked me out of silence." " Follow me, —
It is thyself, — if I must wake from this,
'Twill be to death or madness. Follow me,
From darkness palpable, to earth, to light
Of ample skies, and freshness of blown grass
And rolling waters." " Hold ! " the jarring voice
Of Ades interposed: " 'Tis excellent
The attribute we gave thee, to convert
To such a weapon as may overcome
The old hereditary foes of man,
Sleep, death, corruption, and necessity.
But to reveal thyself the peer of gods,
Not only through inspired ecstasy,
But through a continent persistency,
This never was accomplished by thy race,
And thou must yet be tried. This soul is thine,
For thou hast won her from the jaws of Hell;

Yea, she may follow thee as free as light, —
Lead thou the way and charm the hostile fiends.
Look forward ever; if thine eyes revert
But once to gaze on her, to reassure
Unworthy fears, or sate a mean desire,
Thou art not mate for us. She will dissolve
To empty air — never to be recalled.

ORPHEUS.

Back to the vital earth, O follow me,
    Regained Eurydice.
To rippling well-heads and to sunlit plains,
    Greened by soft wash of rains.
See orchards rosy with prolific bloom,
    And vineyards' purple gloom.
Lulled by the languid flow of lilied streams,
    There will I sing my dreams.
Behold! I chant a hymn of adoration,
    Triumphant exultation,
For I can see, in all the universe,
    No error and no curse.
The gods have naught withheld, in power and sway,
    From him who will obey
Their own divine and everlasting laws.
    Above the world's applause,
As vigorous as morning, he can rise,
    Wrest the desired prize

From the clenched hands of Nemesis and Fate.
    With victory elate,
I chant unmitigated prayer and praise
    To gods who part our ways,
Seeing 'midst clamorous change incredible,
    That all is ordered well.
In more harmonious strains, O lyre, express
    My twice-born happiness;
Yea, utter and translate with larger sense
    My rich experience,
That makes complete life's solemn threnody
    Joy unalloyed and free,
Grief unexampled, victory at last,
    When strife is overpast.

Through pathways hedged with horrors still they
    fared
Invulnerable. Darkness stayed them not,
Nor yet more dreadful light, revealing oft
The hideous fiends who rose on every side,
Huge shapes of ill, to gaze upon the twain.
A Greek, who, fleeing, smote a vibrant lyre,
That chimed to carols more divinely quired
Than those that fill with ravishment a grove,
Misty with moonlight, where the plain brown bird

Makes midnight vocal. Closely following him,
A woman with grave aspect, parted lips,
Upraising, in enthrallèd ecstasy,
Large eyes serene, fulfilled with holier light
For having pierced beyond the boundaries
Of time and of mortality. The day
Shone through the murk at last, and filled their path
With dusky sunbeams; and far-stretching fields
Of soft, delicious green, and crystal skies,
Encouraged them; all perils past save one.
But a black, stagnant river crawled along,
Spanned by no bridge, and ferried by no sail,
With muddy tide between the day and them.
And Orpheus with enamored eyes passed on,
And saw not how the loathsome waters crept,
Nor how his magic song enchanted them
To solid substance; but he missed at once
The footsteps light that had inspired his lay.
Imupetous he turned to reassure
His fearful soul, and sate his hungry eyes;
But as he turned, the inspiration fled,
His lips refused to frame the fruitless words,
His eyes beheld,—O gods! Eurydice
Removed already far away from him,
By all the wide-expanded space, between
Our loftiest dream and our unworthy deed.

She gazed with no reproachful glance nor tears,
And Orpheus felt himself beneath her, fall,
Momently down from empyreal heights,
And lo! he stood within the fields of Thrace,
On earth familiar, 'neath familiar skies,
And heard a voice float through the shining air,
From unimaginable distances,
Faint as a dream, — " Farewell, farewell, farewell."

" Woe! woe! what lamentations may express
The fullness of my new calamity!
I, overbearing, who presumed to reach
The lordly and severe stability
Of the immortals, — whom may I invoke?
To whom may man appeal when he hath failed
Unto himself? What god will interpose
To thwart invincible necessity?
Lost, lost forever! I stood elevate,
For one brief moment dreaming I had won
The skill and power of true divinity.
Gods! with what lofty and superb disdain
Ye must look down on mine unworthy haste, —
Ye, who with grandeur of sublime repose,
And majesty of patience, still abide
Invariable through eternity!

Alas! my mighty visions were to me
Auspicious omens, and they fed my heart
With vigor and encouragement; but now,
This was no dream; for Hope, full-flushed and fair,
Born, like the freshness of auroral dew,
From unseen air, and traceless vanishing,
Consorts not with this mighty goddess, Truth,
With solemn and unfathomable eyes,
For Truth is one with Death and Destiny.
With what a depth of meaning didst thou turn,
For the last time, to me, Eurydice,
A glory 'midst the darkness, with that glance
Of infinite compassion, hands outstretched,
As if to save me from mine own defect.
With what humiliation and despair
I saw thee rising unattainably! —
The vault, the stream accursed had disappeared;
I was in Thrace uplooking to the sky.
O, to what harmonies I might have wed
The blessed tidings which all men await!
Now I can only make my song express
A distant echo, a suggestion vague,
Of the serene contentment of thy voice.
Sing this, my lyre, that all who hark to thee
With an attentive and a gentle ear,
May hear the promise, faint and yet assured,
Recall the grace and the deliciousness

Of immortality, and strive anew
Towards the ideal unattained by me,
Yet still accessible to stronger souls."
Thus Orpheus, when the first wild burst of woe
Had passed; no need to seek her now;
No need to wander o'er the peopled earth.
Was he in truth a victim of the gods,
Or rather with a fairer fortune blest
Than happier men, selected for a fate
Divinely tragical, that he might know
The fullness of a life's experience,
And find expression adequate for all,
Simple as wisdom, and as dignified
As silence? From his kind he lived apart,
As one who cherishes a grief, nor seeks
Forgetfulness nor comfort; elevate
To glittering eminence by destiny,
And lonely through the privacy of woe
Beyond the reaches of man's sympathy.
Where lucid Hebrus bathes its golden sands,
He sat discoursing gracious harmonies,
Amidst the morning fields, when on his ears
Sounded with horrid dissonance the clang
Of smitten cymbals and the throb of drums.
But still the revelers remained unseen,
Till, rounding suddenly a neighboring hill,
The whole mad troop came dancing into sight.

First marched a jovial bacchanal, who bore
A crystal vessel, decked with branching vine,
Then youth and nymphs with ivy chapleted,
In purfled raiment of hues delicate,
With mitres, thyrsi, cymbals, drums and flutes,
Some balancing upon their graceful heads,
Regal with crisp-curled gold, their burdens light
Of baskets heaped with figs and dusky grapes.
And 'midst them all the sacrificial goat,
Adorned with berries. Thus the festal throng,
With wanton gestures, and with antic bounds,
And wild embracings, mad with wine, approached,
With peals of laughter, echoing faintly back
From jocund hill to hill, and lusty shouts
Of " Bacché, Bacché! "

SONG.

With wassail all the night,
Celestial Bacchus, we have worshipped thee!
With riotous revel and with festal wine.
Still on the hills in early morning light,
With frolic dances and brisk jollity,
  Our hymns of praise are thine.

For we have seen thee, god!
The fawn-skin slipping from thy shoulder bare,
Thy gestures lithe and loose, thine eyes that shine,
Thy rosy hands that waved a clustered rod

Of uncrushed grapes, and thine ambrosial hair,
　　Dripping with myrrh and wine.

　　Thou art not strict, severe,
Like loftier gods and ruthless goddesses,
Implacable like Pallas, Zeus, or Truth;
But to humanity akin and near,
Eager for folly, and the luxuries
　　Of lustful health and youth.

　　This crystal-vialed balm,
Divinely brewed, soothing as Lethe's streams,
Is the most generous gift of Deity,
Informing us with soft oblivion calm
Of Death and Fate, with joys beyond the dreams
　　Of grave sobriety.

　　Come, let us drink again.
Resound, O timbrels, and thou bird-voiced flute;
Thyrsus and pipes make shrill and clear acclaim,
To Bacchus, who impurples hill and plain
With vineyards bursting with increase of fruit,
　　Subtle as liquid flame.

　　Œvoë! quaff and sing!
Who drinks no more, offends the deity
Of Bacchus! lo on Hebrus' grassy brink,
A minstrel sits, with gold lute glistening,

Marring our rites with stern solemnity,
    Who doth not chant nor drink.

    Ho! Orpheus, laugh again,
From mirthful heart, and join our happy throng;
Cease to lament with unappeased desire.
We bring a cordial for all grief and pain.
Add to the choral strain thy siren song,
    And thine enchanted lyre.

    For Fate hath answered thee
With cold derision; Death respondeth not.
Here is a god who soothes the soul and sense
With sweet nepenthe, — thy Eurydice
Thou wilt not lure to earthly grove nor grot
    With suasive eloquence.

    Here, nymphs no whit less fair
Are waiting thee, with warm, caressing arms
And loving eyes, lips fit for gods to kiss,
And rosy shoulders, dimpling white and bare, —
Pliant and graceful, with innumerous charms,
    To sate thy heart with bliss.

ORPHEUS.

Hence, thou ignoble throng!
Dare ye profane the splendid purity,

The high nobility of morn, with rites
Lewd and disgusting, and delirious song,
Completing in clear sunshine, shamelessly,
    Rude orgies of wild nights?

BACCHANTES.

    Ha! he insults the god,
With his presumptuous and impious scorn.
Avenge, O bacchanals, the cause divine;
Compel him with the sacred cup and rod,
To quaff his salutation to the morn,
    In frothing, Massic wine!

ORPHEUS.

    Mad bacchanals, begone!
I honor all the gods and Nemesis.
They favor not such frantic revelry,
But blameless lives, and deeds most like their own,
The service of a patient heart submiss,
    And staunch integrity.

    Behold the morning hills,
Sky-kissed Libethra, delicate as air;
The fragile grasses gray with wreaths of dew.
Hark to the tumbling of the mountain rills
To Eos and Athene your first prayer
    And sacrifice are due.

BACCHANTES.

With shameless blasphemy,
He dares proscribe, O god, thy rank and fame.
Enough! enough! he hath despised us long,
Bewailing his beloved Eurydice.
O nymphs,* avenge yourselves in Liber's name,
    Slay him 'midst dance and song.

Your deadly javelins fling
With flinty missiles at the singer proud,
Who deems himself an equal of the gods,
Because he hath the skill to pipe and sing,
With facile fluency of speech endowed.
    Smite him with spears and rods.

ORPHEUS.

Ring forth, my lyre, again, —
With magic harmonies my doom avert,
In tones as plaintive and as rich as life.

BACCHANTES.

Our stones and javelins we have hurled in vain;
His lyre enchants them, he remains unhurt,
    'Midst all the wrath and strife.

Toss the loud tambourine,
Its tight-drawn skin with noisy fingers smite;

Clash ye the cymbals, sing with fatal art;
Cast ye his sundered limbs the stream within, —
They irritate us, soft and bare and white;
    Rend them, O nymphs, apart.

ORPHEUS.

    Sweet Death, deliver me
Out of the reach of envy, lust, and hate;
Enfold me in thy large-embracing arms.

BACCHANTES.

Ah! will he now invoke Eurydice,
Madly resisting his allotted fate
    With vile, unhallowed charms?

    So with a clamorous swell
Of drums and timbrels, we o'erpower the breath
Of dulcet and persuasive melody.

ORPHEUS.

The maniacs conquer! O my lyre, farewell!
Approach, thou beautiful and welcome Death,
    With lost Eurydice.

December 2, 1869.

LOHENGRIN.

———◆———

TO MY COUSIN WASHINGTON.

1870

LOHENGRIN.

PROEM.

THE alert and valiant faith that could respond,
    Upon life's threshold, to the highest call,
    Unquestioning of what might lie beyond, —
Courage afield and courtesy in hall,
And sweet, unbroken patience therewithal,
And simple loyalty, — can these things be
The virtues that have died with chivalry?

The lapsing stream that leads to love and fate,
    Now mystic-shadowed, and now broad and free,
Reflecting all the gold of heaven's gate;
    The snowy bird's symbolic purity,
    The toilsome contest and the victory,
The troubled joy of life, and after these,
The crowning guerdon of the perfect peace, —

These dreams have filled my dazzled sense and
    brain,
  With images so vivid that at last
I wake to life and find them all again
  Repeated in the present as the past,
  The hues recolored and the forms recast;
And in familiar eyes I see outshine
The old heroic faith in love divine.

No empty fable of a day long dead,
  No baseless vision of some sanguine saint,
No legend, only half rememberéd,
  Of prowess obsolete and virtues quaint;
  But be this rather a reflection faint
Of that which taught me how the near and real
Surpass in strength and beauty the ideal.

LOHENGRIN.

THE holy bell, untouched by human hands,
Clanged suddenly, and tolled with solemn knell.

Between the massive, blazoned temple-doors,
Thrown wide, to let the summer morning in,
Sir Lohengrin, the youngest of the knights,
Had paused to taste the sweetness of the air.
All sounds came up the mountain-side to him,
Softened to music, — noise of laboring men,
The cheerful cock-crow and the low of kine,
Bleating of sheep, and twittering of the birds,
Commingled into murmurous harmonies —
When harsh, and near, and clamorous tolled the
    bell.
He started, with his hand upon his sword;
His face, an instant since serene and fair,
And simple with the beauty of a boy,
Heroic, flushed, expectant all at once.
The lovely valley stretching out beneath

Was now a painted picture, — nothing more;
All music of the mountain or the vale
Rang meaningless to him who heard the bell.
"I stand upon the threshold, and am called,"
His clear, young voice shrilled gladly through the air,
And backward through the sounding corridors.

"And have ye heard the bell, my brother knights,
Untouched by human hands or winds of heaven?
It called me, yea, it called my very name!"
So, breathing still of morning, Lohengrin
Sprang 'midst the gathering circle of the knights,
Eager, exalted. "Nay, it called us all:
It rang as it hath often rung before, —
Because the good cause, somewhere on the earth,
Requires a champion," with a serious smile,
An elder gravely answered. "Where to go?
We know not, and we know not whom to serve."
Then spake Sir Percivale, their holiest knight,
And father of the young Sir Lohengrin :
"All that to us seems old, familiar, stale,
Unto the boy is vision, miracle.
Cross him not, brethren, in his first desire.
I will dare swear the summons rang to him,
Not sternly solemn, as it tolled to us,

But gracious, sweet, and gay as marriage-bells."
His pious hands above the young man's head
Wandered in blessing, lightly touching it,
As fondly as a mother. " Lohengrin,
My son, farewell, — God send thee faith and strength."
" God send me patience and humility,"
Murmured the boyish knight, from contrite heart,
With head downcast for those anointing hands.
Then raising suddenly wide, innocent eyes, —
" Father, my faith is boundless as God's love."

Complete in glittering silver armor clad,
With silver maiden-shield, blank of device,
Sir Lohengrin rode down the Montsalvatsch,
With Percivale and Tristram, Frimutelle
And Eliduc, to speed him on his quest.
They fared in silence, for the elder knights
Were filled with grave misgivings, solemn thoughts
Of fate and sorrow, and they heard the bell
Tolling incessant; while Sir Lohengrin,
Buoyant with hope, and dreaming like a girl,
With wild blood dancing in his veins, had made
The journey down the mount unconsciously,
Surprised to find that he had reached the vale.
Distinct and bowered in green the mountain loomed,
Topped with the wondrous temple, with its cross

Smitten to splendor by the eastern sun.
Around them lay the valley beautiful,
Imparadised with flowers and light of June;
And through the valley flowed a willowy stream,
Golden and gray, at this delicious hour,
With purity and sunshine. Here the knights,
Irresolute, gave pause, — which path to choose?
" God lead me right! " said meek Sir Lohengrin;
And as he spoke, afar upon the stream,
He saw a shining swan approaching them.
Full-breasted, with the current it sailed down,
Dazzling in sun and shadow, air and wave,
With unseen movement, wings a little spread,
Their downy under-feathers fluttering,
Stirred by its stately progress; in its beak
It held a silver chain, and drew thereby
A dainty carven shallop after it,
Embossed with silver and with ivory.
" Lead ye my charger up the mount again,"
Cried Lohengrin, and leaped unto the ground,
" For I will trust my guidance to the swan."
" Nay, hold, Sir Lohengrin," said Eliduc,
" Thou hast not made provision for this quest."
" God will provide," the pious knight replied.
Then Percival : " Be faithful to thy vows;
Bethink thee of thine oath when thou art asked
Thy mission in the temple, or thy race.

LOHENGRIN.

Farewell, farewell." " Farewell," cried Lohengrin,
And sprang into the shallop as it passed,
And waved farewells unto his brother knights,
Until they saw the white and silver shine
Of boat and swan and armor less and less,
Till in the willowy distance they were lost.

  Skirting the bases of the rolling hills,
He glided on the river hour by hour,
All through the endless summer day. At first
On either side the willows brushed his boat,
Then underneath their sweeping arch he passed,
Into a rich, enchanted wilderness,
Cool, full of mystic shadows and rare lights,
Wherein the very river changed its hue,
Reflecting tender shades of waving green,
And mossy undergrowth of grass and fern.
Here yellow lilies floated 'midst broad leaves,
Upon their reedy stalks, and far below,
Beneath the flags and rushes, coppery bream
Sedately sailed, and flickering perch, and dace
With silvery lustres caught the glancing rays
Of the June sun upon their mottled scales.
'Midst the close sedge the bright-eyed water-mouse
Nibbled its food, while overhead, its kin,
The squirrel, frisked among the trees. The air
Was full of life and sound of restless birds,

Darting with gayer tints of red and blue
And speckled plumage 'mid gray willow leaves,
And sober alders, and light-foliaged birch.
Unnumbered insects fluttered o'er the banks,
Some dimpling the smooth river's slippery floor,
Leaping from point to point.   Then passed the
    knight
'Twixt broad fields basking in excess of light,
And girt around by range on range of hills,
Green, umber, purple, waving limitless,
Unto the radiant crystal of the sky.
Through unfamiliar solitudes the swan ·
Still led him, and he saw no living thing
Save creatures of the wood, no human face,
Nor sign of human dwelling.   But he sailed,
Holding high thoughts and vowing valorous vows,
Filled with vast wonder and keen happiness,
At the world's very beauty, and his life
Opened in spacious vistas measureless,
As lovely as the stream that bore him on.
So dazzled was the boyish Lohengrin
By all the vital beauty of the real,
And the yet wilder beauty of his dreams,
That he had lost all sense of passing time,
And woke as from a trance of centuries,
To find himself within the heart of hills,
The river widened to an ample lake,

And the swan faring towards a narrow gorge,
That seemed to lead him to the sunset clouds.
Suffused with color were the extremest heights;
The river rippled in a glassy flood,
Glorying in the glory of the sky.
O what a moment for a man to take
Down with him in his memory to the grave!
Life at that hour appeared as infinite
As expectation, sacred, wonderful,
A vision and a privilege. The stream
Lessened to force its way through rocky walls,
Then swerved and flowed, a purple brook, through
    woods
Dewy with evening, sunless, odorous.
There Lohengrin, with eyes upon the stream,
Now brighter than the earth, saw, deep and clear,
The delicate splendor of the earliest star.
All night, too full of sweet expectancy,
Too reverent of the loveliness, for sleep,
He watched the rise and setting of the stars.
All things were new upon that magic day,
Suggesting nobler possibilities,
For a life passed in wise serenity,
Confided with sublimely simple faith
Unto the guidance of the higher will.
In the still heavens hung the large round moon,
White on the blue-black ripples glittering,

And rolled soft floods of slumberous, misty light
Over dim fields and colorless, huge hills.
But the pure swan still bore its burden on,
The ivory shallop and the silver knight,
Pale-faced in that white lustre, neither made
For any port, but seemed to float at will
Aimlessly in a strange, unpeopled land.
So passed the short fair night, and morning broke
Upon the river where it flowed through flats
Wide, fresh, and vague in gray, uncertain dawn,
With cool air sweet from leagues of dewy grass.
Then 'midst the flush and beauty of the east,
The risen sun made all the river flow,
Smitten with light, in gold and gray again.
Rightly he judged his voyage but begun,
When the swan loitered by low banks set thick
With cresses, and red berries, and sweet herbs,
That he might pluck and taste thereof; for these
Such wondrous vigor in his frame infused,
They seemed enchanted and ambrosial fruits.
Day waxed and waned and vanished many times,
And many suns still found him journeying;
But when the sixth night darkened hill and wold,
He seemed bewitched as by a wizard's spell,
By this slow, constant progress, and deep sleep
Possessed his spirit, and his head drooped low
On the hard pillow of his silver shield.

Unconscious he was borne through silent hours,
Nor wakened by the dawn of a new day,
But in his dreamless sleep he never lost
The sense of moving forward on a stream.
Now fared the swan through tilled and cultured lands,
Dappled with sheep and kine on pastures soft,
Sprinkled with trim and pleasant cottages,
With men and women working noiselessly,
As in a picture; nearer then they drew,
And sounds of rural labor, spoken words,
Sir Lohengrin might hear, but still he slept,
Nor saw the shining turrets of a town,
Gardens and castles, domes and cross-topped spires
Fair in the distance, and the flowing stream,
Cleaving its liquid path 'midst many men,
And glittering galleries filled with courtly folk,
Ranged for a tourney-show in open air.
Ah! what a miracle it seemed to these, —
The white bird bearing on the river's breast
That curious, sparkling shallop, and within
The knight in silver armor, with bared head,
And crisp hair blown about his angel face,
Asleep upon his shield! They gazed on him
As on the incarnate spirit of pure faith,
And as the very ministrant of God.
But one great damsel throned beside a king,

With coroneted head and white, wan face,
Flushed suddenly, and clasped her hands in prayer,
And raised large, lucid eyes in thanks to Heaven.
Then, in his dreamless slumber, Lohengrin,
Feeling the steady motion of the boat
Suddenly cease, awoke. Refreshed, alert,
He knew at once that he had reached his port,
And saw that peerless maiden thanking Heaven
For his own advent, and his heart leaped up
Into his throat, and love o'ermastered him.
After the blare of flourished trumpets died,
A herald thus proclaimed the tournament:
" Greetings and glory to the majesty
Of the imperial Henry. By his grace,
This tourney has been granted to the knight,
Frederick of Telramund, who claims the hand
Of Lady Elsie, Duchess of Brabant,
His ward, and stands prepared to prove in arms
His rights against all champions in the lists,
Whom his unwilling mistress may select.
Sir Frederick, Lord of Telramund, is here :'
What champion will espouse the lady's cause?"
Sir Frederick, huge in stature and in bulk,
In gleaming armor terribly equipped,
Advanced defiant, as the herald ceased.
Then Lohengrin, with spear and shield in hand,
Sprang lightly, from his shallop, in the lists.

His beaver raised disclosed his ardent face,
His whole soul shining from inspired eyes.
With cast-back head, sun-smitten silver mail,
Quivering with spirit, light, and life, he stood,
And flung his gauntlet at Sir Frederick's feet,
Crying with shrill, clear voice that rang again,
" Sir Lohengrin adopts the lady's cause."
Then these with shock of conflict couched their spears
In deadly combat; but their weapons clanged
Harmless against their mail impregnable,
Or else were nimbly foiled by dexterous shields.
Unequal and unjust it seemed at first, —
The slender boy matched with the warrior huge,
Who bore upon him with the skill and strength
Of a tried conqueror; but the stranger knight
Displayed such agile grace in parrying blows,
Such fiery valor dealing his own strokes,
That men looked on in wonder, and his foe
Was hardly put upon it for his life.
Thrice they gave pause, to breathe, and to prepare
For fiercer battle, and the galleries rang
With plaudits, and the names of both the knights.
And they, with spirits whetted by the strife,
Met for the fourth, last time, and fenced and struck,
And the keen lance of Lohengrin made way,

Between the meshes of Sir Frederick's mail,
Through cuirass and through jerkin, to the flesh,
With pain so sharp and sudden that he fell.
Then Henry threw his warder to the ground,
And cried the stranger knight had won the day;
And all the lesser voices, following his,
Called, " Lohengrin — Sir Lohengrin hath won ! "
He, flushed with victory, standing in the lists,
Deafened with clamor of his very name,
Reëchoed to the heavens, felt himself
Alone and alien, and would fain float back
Unto the temple, had he not recalled
The fair, great damsel throned beside the king.
But lo! the swan had vanished, and the boat
He fancied he descried a tiny star,
Glimmering in the shining distances.
" His Majesty would greet Sir Lohengrin ;
And Lady Elsie, Duchess of Brabant,
Would thank him for his prowess." Thus proclaimed
The herald, while the unknown knight was led
To the imperial throne. Then Elsie spake :
" Thou hast redeemed my life from misery ;
How may I worthily reward or thank ?
Be thou the nearest to our ducal throne,
The highest knight of Limburg and Brabant,
The greatest gentleman, — unless thy rank,
In truth, be suited to thine own deserts,

And thou, a prince, art called to higher aims."
"Madam, my thanks are rather due to Fate,
For having chosen so poor an instrument
For such a noble end. A knight am I,
The champion of the helpless and oppressed,
Bound by fast vows to own no other name
Than Lohengrin, the Stranger, in this land,
And to depart when asked my race or rank.
Trusting in God I came, and, trusting Him,
I must remain, for all my fate hath changed,
All my desires and hopes, since I am here."

So ended that great joust, and in the days
Thereafter Elsie and Sir Lohengrin,
United by a circumstance so strange,
Loved and were wedded. A more courteous duke,
A braver chevalier, Brabant ne'er saw.
Such grace breathed from his person and his deeds,
Such simple innocence and faith looked forth
From eyes well-nigh too beautiful for man,
That whom he met, departed as his friend.
But Elsie, bound to him by every bond
Of love and honor and vast gratitude,
Being of lesser faith and confidence,
Tortured herself with envious jealousies,
Misdoubting her own beauty, and her power
To win and to retain so great a heart.

Each year Sir Lohengrin proclaimed a joust
In memory of the tourney where he won
His lovely Duchess, and his lance prevailed
Against all lesser knights. When his twain sons,
Loyal and brave and gentle as their sire,
Had grown to stalwart men, and his one girl,
Eyed like himself and as his Duchess fair,
Floramie, grew to gracious maidenhood,
He gave a noble tourney, and o'erthrew
The terrible and potent Duke of Cleves.
"Ha!" sneered the Dame of Cleves, "this Lohen-
 grin
May be a knight adroit and valorous,
But who knows whence he sprang?" and lightly
 laughed,
Seeing the hot blood kindle Elsie's cheek.
That night Sir Lohengrin sought rest betimes,
By hours of crowded action quite forespent,
And found the Duchess Elsie on her couch,
Staining the silken broideries with her tears.
"Why dost thou weep?" he questioned tenderly,
Kissing her delicate hands, and parting back
Her heavy yellow hair from brow and face.
"The Duchess Anne of Cleves hath wounded me."
"Sweet, am not I at hand to comfort thee?"
And he caressed her as an ailing child,
Until she smiled and slept. But the next night

He found her weeping, and he questioned her,
With the same answer, and again she slept;
Then the third night he asked her why she grieved,
And she uprising, white, with eager eyes,
Cried, "Lohengrin, my lord, my only love,
For our sons' sake, who know not whence they spring,
Our daughter who remains a virgin yet,
Let me not hear folk girding at thy race.
I know thy blood is royal, I have faith;
But tell me all, that I may publish it
Unto our dukedom."   Hurt and wondering,
He answered simply, "I am Lohengrin,
Son to Sir Percivale, and ministrant
Within the holy temple of the Grail.
I would thy faith were greater, this is all.
Now must I bid farewell."   "O Lohengrin,
What have I done?"   She clung about his neck,
And moistened all his beard with streaming tears;
But he with one long kiss relaxed her arms
Calmly from his embrace, and stood alone.
"Blame not thy nature now with vain reproofs.
This also is our fate: in all things else
We have submitted, — let us yield in this,
With no less grace now that God tries our hearts,
Than when He sent us victory and love."
"Yea, go, — you never loved me," faltered she;
"I will not blame my nature, but your own.

Through all our wedded years I doubted you;
Your eyes have never brightened meeting mine
As I have seen them in religious zeal,
Or in exalted hours of victory."
A look of perfect weariness, unmixed
With wrath or grief, o'erspread the knight's pale
 face ;
But with the pity that a god might show
Towards one with ills impossible to him,
He drew anear, caressing her, and sighed:
" Through all our wedded years you doubted me?
Poor child, poor child ! and it has come to this.
Thank Heaven, I gave no cause for your mistrust,
Desiring never an ideal more fair
Of womanhood than was my chosen wife."
She, broken, sobbing, leaned her delicate head
On his great shoulder, and remorseful cried,
" O loyal, honest, simple Lohengrin,
Thy wife has been unworthy : this is why
Thou sayest farewell in accents cold and strange,
With alien eyes that even now behold
Things fairer, better, than her mournful face."
But he with large allowance answered her :
" If this be truth, it is because I feel
That I belong no more unto myself,
Neither to thee, for God withdraws my soul
Beyond all earthly passions unto Him.

Now that we know our doom, with serious calm,
Beside thee I will sit, till break of day,
Thus holding thy chill hand and tell thee all.
This will resign thee, for I cannot think
How any human soul that hath beheld
Life's compensations and its miracles,
Can fail to trust in what is yet to come."
Then he began from that auroral hour
When he first heard the temple bell, and told
The wonder of the swan that came for him,
His journey down the stream, the tournament,
His strength unwonted, combating the knight
Who towered above him with superior force
Of flesh and sinew, — how he prayed through all,
Imploring God to let the just cause win,
Unconscious of the close-thronged galleries,
Feeling two eyes alone that burned his soul.
She knew the rest. Therewith he kissed her brow
And ended, — "Now the knights will take me back
Into the temple; all who keep their vows,
Are welcomed there again to peace and rest.
There will my years fall from me like a cloak,
And I will stand again at manhood's prime.
Then when all errors of the flesh are purged
From these I loved here, they may follow me,
Unto perpetual worship and to peace."
She lay quite calm, and smiling heard his voice,

Already grown to her remote and changed,
And when he ceased, arose and gazed in awe
On his transfigured face and kissed his brow,
And understood, accepting all her fate.
Anon he called his children, and to these:
" Farewell, sweet Florance and dear Percivale;
Here is my horn, and here mine ancient sword, —
Guard them with care and win with them repute.
Here, Elsie, is the ring my mother gave, —
Part with it never; and thou, Floramie,
Take thou my love, — I have naught else to give;
Be of strong faith in him thou mean'st to wed."
So these communed together, till the night
Died from the brightening skies, and in the east
The morning star hung in aerial rose,
And the blue deepened; while moist lawn and hedge
Breathed dewy freshness through the windows oped.
Then on the stream, that nigh the palace flowed,
A stainless swan approached them; in its beak
It held a silver chain, and drew thereby
A dainty, carven shallop after it,
Embossed with silver and with ivory.
Followed by waved farewells and streaming eyes,
Sir Lohengrin embarked and floated forth
Unto perpetual worship and to peace.

TANNHAÜSER.

TO MY MOTHER.

MAY, 1870.

TANNHAÜSER.

THE Landgrave Hermann held a gathering
Of minstrels, minnesingers, troubadours,
At Wartburg in his palace, and the knight,
Sir Tannhaüser of France, the greatest bard,
Inspired with heavenly visions, and endowed
With apprehension and rare utterance
Of noble music, fared in thoughtful wise
Across the Hörsel meadows. Full of light,
And large repose, the peaceful valley lay,
In the late splendor of the afternoon,
And level sunbeams lit the serious face
Of the young knight, who journeyed to the west,
Towards the precipitous and rugged cliffs,
Scarred, grim, and torn with savage rifts and
　　chasms,
That in the distance loomed as soft and fair
And purple as their shadows on the grass.
The tinkling chimes rang out athwart the air,
Proclaiming sunset, ushering evening in,
Although the sky yet glowed with yellow light.

The ploughboy, ere he led his cattle home,
In the near meadow, reverently knelt,
And doffed his cap, and duly crossed his breast,
Whispering his "Ave Mary," as he heard
The pealing vesper-bell. But still the knight,
Unmindful of the sacred hour announced,
Disdainful or unconscious, held his course.
"Would that I also, like yon stupid wight,
Could kneel and hail the Virgin and believe!"
He murmured bitterly beneath his breath.
"Were I a pagan, riding to contend
For the Olympic wreath, O with what zeal,
What fire of inspiration, would I sing
The praises of the gods! How may my lyre
Glorify these whose very life I doubt?
The world is governed by one cruel God,
Who brings a sword, not peace. A pallid Christ,
Unnatural, perfect, and a virgin cold,
They give us for a heaven of living gods,
Beautiful, loving, whose mere names were song;
A creed of suffering and despair, walled in
On every side by brazen boundaries,
That limit the soul's vision and her hope
To a red hell or an unpeopled heaven.
Yea, I am lost already, — even now
Am doomed to flaming torture for my thoughts.
O gods! O gods! where shall my soul find peace?"

He raised his wan face to the faded skies,
Now shadowing into twilight; no response
Came from their sunless heights; no miracle,
As in the ancient days of answering gods.
With a long, shuddering sigh he glanced to earth,
Finding himself among the Hörsel cliffs.
Gray, sullen, gaunt, they towered on either side;
Scant shrubs sucked meagre life between the rifts
Of their huge crags, and made small darker spots
Upon their wrinkled sides; the jaded horse
Stumbled upon loose, rattling, fallen stones,
Amidst the gathering dusk, and blindly fared
Through the weird, perilous pass. As darkness
    waxed,
And an oppressive mystery enwrapped
The roadstead and the rocks, Sir Tannhaüser
Fancied he saw upon the mountain-side
The fluttering of white raiment. With a sense
Of a wild joy and horror, he gave pause,
For his sagacious horse that reeked with sweat,
Trembling in every limb, confirmed his thought,
That nothing human scaled that haunted cliff.
The white thing seemed descending, — now a cloud
It looked, and now a rag of drifted mist,
Torn in the jagged gorge precipitous,
And now an apparition clad in white,
Shapely and real, — then he lost it quite,

Gazing on nothing with blank, foolish face.
As with wide eyes he stood, he was aware
Of a strange splendor at his very side,
A presence and a majesty so great,
That ere he saw, he felt it was divine.
He turned, and, leaping from his horse, fell prone,
In speechless adoration, on the earth,
Before the matchless goddess, who appeared
With no less freshness of immortal youth
Than when first risen from foam of Paphian seas.
He heard delicious strains of melody,
Such as his highest muse had ne'er attained,
Float in the air, while in the distance rang,
Harsh and discordant, jarring with those tones,
The gallop of his frightened horse's hoofs,
Clattering in sudden freedom down the pass.
A voice that made all music dissonance
Then thrilled through heart and flesh of that prone
    knight,
Triumphantly: "The gods need but appear,
And their usurpéd thrones are theirs again!"
Then tenderly: "Sweet knight, I pray thee, rise;
Worship me not, for I desire thy love.
Look on me, follow me, for I am fain
Of thy fair, human face." He rose and looked,
Stirred by that heavenly flattery to the soul.
Her hair, unbraided and unfilleted,

Rained in a glittering shower to the ground,
And cast forth lustre. Round her zone was clasped
The scintillant cestus, stiff with flaming gold,
Thicker with restless gems than heaven with stars.
She might have flung the enchanted wonder forth;
Her eyes, her slightest gesture would suffice
To bind all men in blissful slavery.
She sprang upon the mountain's dangerous side,
With feet that left their print in flowers divine, —
Flushed amaryllis and blue hyacinth,
Impurpled amaranth and asphodel,
Dewy with nectar, and exhaling scents
Richer than all the roses of mid-June.
The knight sped after her, with wild eyes fixed
Upon her brightness, as she lightly leapt
From crag to crag, with flying auburn hair,
Like a gold cloud, that lured him ever on,
Higher and higher up the haunted cliff.
At last amidst a grove of pines she paused,
Until he reached her, breathing hard with haste,
Delight, and wonder. Then upon his hand
She placed her own, and all his blood at once
Tingled and hotly rushed to brow and cheek,
At the supreme caress; but the mere touch
Infused fresh life, and when she looked at him
With gracious tenderness, he felt himself
Strong suddenly to bear the blinding light

Of those great eyes. " Dear knight," she murmured
    low,
" For love of me, wilt thou accord this boon, —
To grace my weary home in banishment ? "
His hungry eyes gave answer ere he spoke,
In tones abrupt that startled his own ears
With their strange harshness; but with thanks
    profuse
She guided him, still holding his cold hand
In her warm, dainty palm, unto a cave,
Whence a rare glory issued, and a smell
Of spice and roses, frankincense and balm.
They entering stood within a marble hall,
With straight, slim pillars, at whose farther end
The goddess led him to a spiral flight
Of stairs, descending always 'midst black gloom
Into the very bowels of the earth.
Down these, with fearful swiftness, they made way,
The knight's feet touching not the solid stair,
But sliding down as in a vexing dream,
Blind, feeling but that hand divine that still
Empowered him to walk on empty air.
Then he was dazzled by a sudden blaze,
In a vast palace filled with reveling folk.
Cunningly pictured on the ivory walls
Were rolling hills, cool lakes, and boscage green,
And all the summer landscape's various pomp.

The precious canopy aloft was carved
In semblance of the pleachéd forest trees,
Enameled with the liveliest green, wherethrough
A light pierced, more resplendent than the day.
O'er the pale, polished jasper of the floor
The goddess led him to a massy throne
Of burnished metal, fretted and embossed,
With all the marvelous story of her birth
Painted in prodigal splendor of rich tincts,
And carved by heavenly artists, — crystal seas,
And long-haired Nereids in their pearly shells,
And all the wonder of her lucent limbs
Sphered in a vermeil mist. Upon the throne
She took her seat, the knight beside her still,
Sinking on couches of fresh asphodel,
And the dance ceased, and the flushed revelers came
In glittering phalanx to adore their queen.
Beautiful girls, with shining delicate heads,
Crested with living jewels, fanned the air
With flickering wings from naked shoulders soft.
Then with preluding low, a thousand harps,
And citherns, and strange nameless instruments,
Sent through the fragrant air sweet symphonies,
And the winged dancers waved in mazy rounds,
With changing lustres like a summer sea.
Fair boys, with charming yellow hair crisp-curled,

And frail, effeminate beauty, the knight saw
But of strong, stalwart men like him were none.
He gazed thereon bewitched, until the hand
Of Venus, erst withdrawn, now fell again
Upon his own, and roused him from his trance.
He looked on her, and as he looked, a cloud
Auroral, flaming as at sunrising,
Arose from nothing, floating over them,
Dropping rich odors, and encircling them
In luminous folds, like that vermilion mist
Penciled upon the throne, and as it waxed
In density and brightness, all the throng
Of festal dancers, less and less distinct,
Grew like pale spirits in a vague, dim dream,
And vanished altogether; and these twain,
Shut from the world in that ambrosial cloud,
Now with a glory inconceivable,
Vivid and conflagrant, looked each on each.

All hours came laden with their own delights
In that enchanted palace, wherein Time
Knew no divisions harsh of night and day,
But light was always, and desire of sleep
Was satisfied at once with slumber soft,
Desire of food with magical repast,
By unseen hands on golden tables spread.
But these the knight accepted like a god,

All less was lost in that excess of joy,
The crowning marvel of her love for him,
Assuring him of his divinity.
Meanwhile remembrance of the earth appeared
Like the vague trouble of a transient dream, —
The doubt, the scruples, the remorse for thoughts
Beyond his own control, the constant thirst
For something fairer than his life, more real
Than airy revelations of his Muse.
Here was his soul's desire satisfied.
All nobler passions died; his lyre he flung
Recklessly forth, with vows to dedicate
His being to herself. She knew and seized
The moment of her mastery, and conveyed
The lyre beyond his sight and memory.
With blandishments divine she changed for him,
Each hour, her mood; a very woman now,
Fantastic, voluble, affectionate,
And jealous of the vague, unbodied air,
Exacting, penitent, and pacified,
All in a breath. And often she appeared
Majestic with celestial wrath, with eyes
That shot forth fire, and a heavy brow,
Portentous as the lowering front of heaven,
When the reverberant, sullen thunder rolls
Among the echoing clouds. Thus she denounced
Her ancient, fickle worshippers, who left

Her altars desecrate, her fires unfed,
Her name forgotten. "But I reign, I reign!"
She would shrill forth, triumphant; "yea, I reign.
Men name me not, but worship me unnamed,
Beauty and Love within their heart of hearts;
Not with bent knees and empty breath of words,
But with devoted sacrifice of lives."
Then melting in a moment, she would weep
Ambrosial tears, pathetic, full of guile,
Accusing her own base ingratitude,
In craving worship, when she had his heart,
Her priceless knight, her peerless paladin,
Her Tannhaüser; then, with an artful glance
Of lovely helplessness, entreated him
Not to desert her, like the faithless world,
For these unbeautiful and barbarous gods,
Or she would never cease her prayers to Jove,
Until he took from her the heavy curse
Of immortality. With closer vows,
The knight then sealed his worship and forswore
All other aims and deeds to serve her cause.
Thus passed unnoted seven barren years
Of reckless passion and voluptuous sloth,
Undignified by any lofty thought
In his degraded mind, that sometime was
Endowed with noble capability.
From revelry to revelry he passed,

Craving more pungent pleasures momently,
And new intoxications; and each hour
The siren goddess answered his desires.
Once when she left him with a weary sense
Of utter lassitude, he sat alone,
And, raising listless eyes, he saw himself
In a great burnished mirror, wrought about
With cunning imagery of twisted vines.
He scarcely knew those sunken, red-rimmed eyes,
And haggard cheeks, and hollow-smiling lips,
For his who in the flush of manhood rode
Among the cliffs, and followed up the crags
The flying temptress; and there fell on him
A horror of her beauty, a disgust
For his degenerate and corrupted life,
With irresistible, intense desire,
To feel the breath of heaven on his face.
Then as Fate willed, who rules above the gods,
He saw, within the glass, behind him glide
The form of Venus. Certain of her power,
She had laid by, in fond security,
The enchanted cestus, and Sir Tannhaüser,
With surfeited regard, beheld her now,
No fairer than the women of the earth,
Whom with serenity and health he left,
Duped by a lovely witch. Before he moved,
She knew her destiny; and when he turned,

He seemed to drop a mask, disclosing thus
An alien face, and eyes with vision true,
That for long time with glamour had been blind.
Hiding the hideous rage within her breast,
With girlish simpleness of folded hands,
Auroral blushes, and sweet, shamefast mien,
She spoke: " Behold, my love, I have cast forth
All magic, blandishments, and sorcery,
For I have dreamed a dream so terrible,
That I awoke to find my pillow stained
With tears as of real woe. I thought my belt,
By Vulcan wrought with matchless skill and power,
Was the sole bond between us; this being doffed,
I seemed to thee an old, unlovely crone,
Wrinkled by every year that I have seen.
Thou turnedst from me with a brutal sneer,
So that I woke with weeping. Then I rose,
And drew the glittering girdle from my zone,
Jealous thereof, yet full of fears, and said,
'If it be this he loves, then let him go!
I have no solace as a mortal hath,
No hope of change or death to comfort me
Through all eternity; yet he is free,
Though I could hold him fast with heavy chains,
Bound in perpetual imprisonment.'
Tell me my vision was a baseless dream;
See, I am kneeling, and I kiss thy hands, —

In pity, look on me, before thy word
Condemns me to immortal misery!"
As he looked down, the infernal influence
Worked on his soul again; for she was fair
Beyond imagination, and her brow
Seemed luminous with high self-sacrifice.
He bent and kissed her head, warm, shining, soft,
With its close-curling gold, and love revived.
But ere he spoke, he heard the distant sound
Of one sweet, smitten lyre, and a gleam
Of violent anger flashed across the face
Upraised to his in feigned simplicity
And singleness of purpose. Then he sprang,
Well-nigh a god himself, with sudden strength
To vanquish and resist, beyond her reach,
Crying, "My old Muse calls me, and I hear!
Thy fateful vision is no baseless dream;
I will be gone from this accursed hall!"
Then she, too, rose, dilating over him,
And sullen clouds veiled all her rosy limbs,
Unto her girdle, and her head appeared
Refulgent, and her voice rang wrathfully:
"Have I cajoled and flattered thee till now,
To lose thee thus! How wilt thou make escape?
Once being mine, thou art forever mine:
Yea, not my love, but my poor slave and fool."
But he, with both hands pressed upon his eyes,

Against that blinding lustre, heeded not
Her thundered words, and cried in sharp despair,
" Help me, O Virgin Mary!" and thereat,
The very bases of the hall gave way,
The roof was rived, the goddess disappeared,
And Tannhaüser stood free upon the cliff,
Amidst the morning sunshine and fresh air.

Around him were the tumbled blocks and crags,
Huge ridges and sharp juts of flinty peaks,
Black caves, and masses of the grim, bald rock.
The ethereal, unfathomable sky
Hung over him, the valley lay beneath,
Dotted with yellow hayricks, that exhaled
Sweet, healthy odors to the mountain-top.
He breathed intoxicate the infinite air,
And plucked the heather blossoms where they blew,
Reckless with light and dew, in crannies green,
And scarcely saw their darling bells for tears.
No sounds of labor reached him from the farms,
And hamlets trim, nor from the furrowed glebe;
But a serene and sabbath stillness reigned,
Till broken by the faint, melodious chimes
Of the small village church that called to prayer.
He hurried down the rugged, scarpéd cliff,
And swung himself from shelving granite slopes
To narrow foot-holds, near wide-throated chasms,

Tearing against sharp stones his bleeding hands,
With long hair flying from his dripping brow,
Uncovered head, and white, exalted face.
No memory had he of his smooth ascent,
No thought of fear upon those dreadful hills;
He only heard the bell, inviting him
To satisfy the craving of his heart,
For worship 'midst his fellow-men. He reached
The beaten, dusty road, and passed thereon
The pious peasants faring towards the church,
And scarce refrained from greeting them like friends
Dearly beloved, after long absence met.
How more than fair the sunburnt wenches looked,
In their rough, homespun gowns and coifs demure,
After the beauty of bare, rosy limbs,
And odorous, loose hair! He noted not
Suspicious glances on his garb uncouth,
His air extravagant and face distraught,
With bursts of laughter from the red-cheeked boys,
And prudent crossings of the women's breasts.
He passed the flowering close about the church,
And trod the well-worn path, with throbbing heart,
The little heather-bell between his lips,
And his eyes fastened on the good green grass.
Thus entered he the sanctuary, lit
With frequent tapers, and with sunbeams stained
Through painted glass. How pure and innocent

The waiting congregation seemed to him,
Kneeling, or seated with calm brows upraised!
With faltering strength, he cowered down alone,
And held sincere communion with the Lord,
For one brief moment, in a sudden gush
Of blessèd tears. The minister of God
Rose to invoke a blessing on his flock,
And then began the service, — not in words
To raise the lowly, and to heal the sick,
But in an alien tongue, with phrases formed,
And meaningless observances. The knight,
Unmoved, yet thirsting for the simple word
That might have moved him, held his bitter thoughts,
But when in his own speech a new priest spake,
Looked up with hope revived, and heard the text :
" Go, preach the Gospel unto all the world.
He that believes and is baptized, is saved.
He that believeth not, is damned in hell!"
He sat with neck thrust forth and staring eyes;
The crowded congregation disappeared;
He felt alone in some black sea of hell,
While a great light smote one exalted face,
Vivid already with prophetic fire,
Whose fatal mouth now thundered forth his doom.
He longed in that void circle to cry out,
With one clear shriek, but sense and voice seemed
  bound,

And his parched tongue clave useless to his mouth.
As the last words resounded through the church,
And once again the pastor blessed his flock,
Who, serious and subdued, passed slowly down
The narrow aisle, none noted, near the wall,
A fallen man with face upon his knees,
A heap of huddled garments and loose hair,
Unconscious 'mid the rustling, murmurous stir,
'Midst light and rural smell of grass and flowers,
Let in athwart the doorway. One lone priest,
Darkening the altar lights, moved noiselessly,
Now with the yellow glow upon his face,
Now a black shadow gliding farther on,
Amidst the smooth, slim pillars of hewn ash.
But from the vacant aisles he heard at once
A hollow sigh, heaved from a depth profound.
Upholding his last light above his head,
And peering eagerly amidst the stalls,
He cried, "Be blest who cometh in God's name."
Then the gaunt form of Tannhaüser arose.
"Father, I am a sinner, and I seek
Forgiveness and help, by whatso means
I can regain the joy of peace with God."
" The Lord hath mercy on the penitent.
' Although thy sins be scarlet,' He hath said,
' Will I not make them white as wool?' Confess,
And I will shrive you." Thus the good priest
    moved

Towards the remorseful knight and pressed his
    hand.
But shrinking down, he drew his fingers back
From the kind palm, and kissed the friar's feet.
" Thy pure hand is anointed, and can heal.
The cool, calm pressure brings back sanity,
And what serene, past joys! yet touch me not,
My contact is pollution, — hear, O hear,
While I disburden my charged soul." He lay,
Casting about for words and strength to speak.
" O Father, is there help for such a one,"
In tones of deep abasement he began,
" Who hath rebelled against the laws of God,
With pride no less presumptuous than his
Who lost thereby his rank in heaven?" "My son
There is atonement for all sins, — or slight
Or difficult, proportioned to the crime.
Though this may be the staining of thy hands
With blood of kinsmen or of fellow-men."
" My hands are white, — my crime hath found no
    name,
This side of hell; yet though my heart-strings snap
To live it over, let me make attempt.
I was a knight and bard, with such a gift
Of revelation that no hour of life
    Lacked beauty and adornment, in myself
    The seat and centre of all happiness.

What inspiration could my lofty Muse
Draw from those common and familiar themes,
Painted upon the windows and the walls
Of every church, — the mother and her child,
The miracle and mystery of the birth,
The death, the resurrection ? Fool and blind !
That saw not symbols of eternal truth
In that grand tragedy and victory,
Significant and infinite as life.
What tortures did my skeptic soul endure,
At war against herself and all mankind !
The restless nights of feverish sleeplessness,
With balancing of reasons nicely weighed;
The dawn that brought no hope nor energy,
The blasphemous arraignment of the Lord,
Taxing His glorious divinity
With all the grief and folly of the world.
Then came relapses into abject fear,
And hollow prayer and praise from craven heart.
Before a sculptured Venus I would kneel,
Crown her with flowers, worship her, and cry,
' O large and noble type of our ideal,
At least my heart and prayer return to thee,
Amidst a faithless world of proselytes.
Madonna Mary, with her virgin lips,
And eyes that look perpetual reproach,
Insults and is a blasphemy on youth.

Is she to claim the worship of a man
Hot with the first rich flush of ripened life?'
Realities, like phantoms, glided by,
Unnoted 'midst the torments and delights
Of my conflicting spirit, and I doffed
The modest Christian weeds of charity
And fit humility, and steeled myself
In pagan panoply of stoicism
And self-sufficing pride. Yet constantly
I gained men's charmed attention and applause,
With the wild strains I smote from out my lyre,
To me the native language of my soul,
To them attractive and miraculous,
As all things whose solution and whose source
Remain a mystery. Then came suddenly
The summons to attend the gathering
Of minstrels at the Landgrave Hermann's court.
Resolved to publish there my pagan creed
In harmonies so high and beautiful
That all the world would share my zeal and faith,
I journeyed towards the haunted Hörsel cliffs.
O God! how may I tell you how *she* came,
The temptress of a hundred centuries,
Yet fresh as April? She bewitched my sense,
Poisoned my judgment with sweet flatteries,
And for I may not guess how many years
Held me a captive in degrading bonds.

There is no sin of lust so lewd and foul,
Which I learned not in that alluring hell,
Until this morn, I snapped the ignoble tie,
By calling on the Mother of our Lord.
O for the power to stand again erect,
And look men in the eyes! What penitence,
What scourging of the flesh, what rigid fasts,
What terrible privations may suffice
To cleanse me in the sight of God and man?"
Ill-omened silence followed his appeal.
Patient and motionless he lay awhile,
Then sprang unto his feet with sudden force,
Confronting in his breathless vehemence,
With palpitating heart, the timid priest.
"Answer me, as you hope for a response,
One day, at the great judgment-seat yourself."
" I cannot answer," said the simple priest,
" I have not understood." "Just God! is this
The curse Thou layest upon me? I outstrip
The sympathy and brotherhood of men,
So far removed is my experience
From their clean innocence. Inspire me,
Prompt me to words that bring me near to them!
Father," in gentler accents he resumed,
"Thank Heaven at your every orison
That sin like mine, you cannot apprehend.
More than the truth perchance I have confessed,

But I have sinned, and darkly, — this is true;
And I have suffered, and am suffering now.
Is there no help in your great Christian creed
Of liberal charity, for such a one?"
"My son," the priest replied, "your speech distraught
Hath quite bewildered me. I fain would hope
That Christ's large charity can reach your sin,
But I know naught. I cannot but believe
That the enchantress who first tempted you
Must be the Evil one, — your early doubt
Was the possession of your soul by him.
Travel across the mountain to the town,
The first cathedral town upon the road
That leads to Rome, — a sage and reverend priest,
The Bishop Adrian, bides there. Say you have come
From his leal servant, Friar Lodovick;
He hath vast lore and great authority,
And may absolve you freely of your sin."

Over the rolling hills, through summer fields,
By noisy villages and lonely lanes,
Through glowing days, when all the landscape
    stretched
Shimmering in the heat, a pilgrim fared
Towards the cathedral town. Sir Tannhaüser
Had donned the mournful sackcloth, girt his loins

With a coarse rope that ate into his flesh,
Muffled a cowl about his shaven head,
Hung a great leaden cross around his neck;
And bearing in his hands a knotty staff,
With swollen, sandaled feet he held his course.
He snatched scant rest at twilight or at dawn,
When his forced travel was least difficult.
But most he journeyed when the sky, o'ercast,
Uprolled its threatening clouds of dusky blue,
And angry thunder grumbled through the hills,
And earth grew dark at noonday, till the flash
Of the thin lightning through the wide sky leapt,
And tumbling showers scoured along the plain.
Then folk who saw the pilgrim penitent,
Drenched, weird, and hastening as to some strange
    doom,
Swore that the wandering Jew had crossed their
    land,
And the Lord Christ had sent the deadly bolt
Harmless upon his cursed, immortal head.
At length the hill-side city's spires and roofs,
With all its western windows smitten red
By a rich sunset, and with massive towers
Of its cathedral overtopping all,
Greeted his sight. Some weary paces more,
And as the twilight deepened in the streets,
He stood within the minster. How serene,

In sculptured calm of centuries, it seemed!
How cool and spacious all the dim-lit aisles,
Still hazy with the fumes of frankincense!
The vesper had been said, yet here and there
A wrinkled beldam, or a mourner veiled,
Or burly burgher on the cold floor knelt,
And still the organist, with wandering hands,
Drew from the keys mysterious melodies,
And filled the church with flying waifs of song,
That with ethereal beauty moved the soul
To a more tender prayer and gentler faith
Than choral anthems and the solemn mass.
A thousand memories, sweet to bitterness,
Rushed on the knight and filled his eyes with tears;
Youth's blamelessness and faith forever lost,
The love of his neglected lyre, his art,
Revived by these aerial harmonies.
He was unworthy now to touch the strings,
Too base to stir men's soul to ecstasy
And high resolves, as in the days agone;
And yet, with all his spirit's earnestness,
He yearned to feel the lyre between his hands,
To utter all the trouble of his life
Unto the Muse who understands and helps.
Outworn with travel, soothed to drowsiness
By dying music and sweet-scented air,

His limbs relaxed, and sleep possessed his frame.
Auroral light the eastern oriels touched,
When with delicious sense of rest he woke,
Amidst the vast and silent empty aisles.
" God's peace hath fallen upon me in this place;
This is my Bethel; here I feel again
A holy calm, if not of innocence,
Yet purest after that, the calm serene
Of expiation and forgiveness."
He spake, and passed with staff and wallet forth
Through the tall portal to the open square,
And turning, paused to look upon the pile.
The northern front against the crystal sky
Loomed dark and heavy, full of sombre shade,
With each projecting buttress, carven cross,
Gable and mullion, tipped with laughing light
By the slant sunbeams of the risen morn.
The noisy swallows wheeled above their nests,
Builded in hidden nooks about the porch.
No human life was stirring in the square,
Save now and then a rumbling market-team,
Fresh from the fields and farms without the town.
He knelt upon the broad cathedral steps,
And kissed the moistened stone, while overhead
The circling swallows sang, and all around
The mighty city lay asleep and still.

    To stranger's ears must yet again be made

The terrible confession; yet again
A deathly chill, with something worse than fear,
Seized the knight's heart, who knew his every word
Widened the gulf between his kind and him.
The Bishop sat with pomp of mitred head,
In pride of proven virtue, hearkening all
With cold, official apathy, nor made
A sign of pity nor encouragement.
The friar understood the pilgrim's grief,
The language of his eyes; his speech alone
Was alien to these kind, untutored ears.
But this was truly to be misconstrued,
To tear each palpitating word alive
From out the depths of his remorseful soul,
And have it weighed with the precision cool
And the nice logic of a reasoning mind.
This spiritual Father judged his crime
As the mad mischief of a reckless boy,
That called for strict, immediate punishment.
But Tannhaüser, who felt himself a man,
Though base, yet fallen through passions and rare gifts
Of an exuberant nature rankly rich,
And knew his weary head was growing gray
With a life's terrible experience,
Found his old sense of proper worth revive;
But modestly he ended: " Yet I felt,

O holy Father, in the church, this morn,
A strange security, a peace serene,
As though e'en yet the Lord regarded me
With merciful compassion; yea, as though
Even so vile a worm as I might work
Mine own salvation, through repentant prayers."
"Presumptuous man, it is no easy task
To expiate such sin; a space of prayer
That deprecates the anger of the Lord,
A pilgrimage through pleasant, summer lands,
May not atone for years of impious lust;
Thy heart hath lied to thee in offering hope."
"Is there no hope on earth?" the pilgrim sighed.
"None through thy penance," said the saintly man.
"Yet there may be through mediation, help.
There is a man who by a blameless life
Hath won the right to intercede with God.
No sins of his own flesh hath he to purge, —
The Cardinal Filippo, — he abides,
Within the Holy City. Seek him out;
This is my only counsel, — through thyself
Can be no help and no forgiveness."

How different from the buoyant joy of morn
Was this discouraged sense of lassitude,
Wherewith the pilgrim, 'midst a summer rain,
Pursued his progress through the cheerless squares!

The Bishop's words were ringing in his ears,
Measured and pitiless, and, blent with these,
The memory of the goddess' last wild cry, —
" *Once being mine, thou art forever mine.*"
Was it the truth, despite his penitence,
And dedication of his thought to God,
That still some portion of himself was hers,
Some lust survived, some criminal regret,
For her corrupted love? He searched his heart:
All was remorse, religious and sincere,
And yet her dreadful curse still haunted him;
For all men shunned him, and denied him help,
Knowing at once in looking on his face,
Ploughed with deep lines and prematurely old,
That he had struggled with some deadly fiend,
And that he was no longer kin to them.
Just past the outskirts of the town, he stopped,
To strengthen will and courage to proceed.
The storm had broken o'er the sultry streets,
But now the lessening clouds were flying east,
And though the gentle shower still wet his face,
The west was cloudless while the sun went down,
And the bright seven-colored arch stood forth,
Against the opposite dull gray. There was
A beauty in the mingled storm and peace,
Beyond clear sunshine, as the vast, green fields
Basked in soft light, though glistening yet with
    rain.

The roar of all the town was now a buzz
Less than the insects' drowsy murmuring
That whirred their gauzy wings around his head.
The breeze that follows on the sunsetting
Was blowing whiffs of bruised and dripping grass
Into the heated city. But he stood,
Disconsolate with thoughts of fate and sin,
Still wrestling with his soul to win it back
From her who claimed it to eternity.
Then on the delicate air there came to him
The intonation of the minster bells,
Chiming the vespers, musical and faint.
He knew not what of dear and beautiful
There was in those familiar peals, that spake
Of his first boyhood and his innocence,
Leading him back, with gracious influence,
To pleasant thoughts and tender memories,
And last, recalling the fair hour of hope
He passed that morning in the church. Again,
The glad assurance of God's boundless love
Filled all his being, and he rose serene,
And journeyed forward with a calm content.

Southward he wended, and the landscape took
A warmer tone, the sky a richer light.
The gardens of the graceful, festooned hops,
With their slight tendrils binding pole to pole,

Gave place to orchards and the trellised grape.
The hedges were enwreathed with trailing vines,
With clustering, shapely bunches, 'midst the growth
Of tangled greenery. The elm and ash
Less frequent grew than cactus, cypresses,
And golden-fruited or large-blossomed trees.
The far hills took the hue of the dove's breast,
Veiled in gray mist of olive groves. No more
He passed dark, moated strongholds of grim knights,
But terraces with marble-paven steps,
With fountains leaping in the sunny air,
And hanging gardens full of sumptuous bloom.
Then cloisters guarded by their dead gray walls,
Where now and then a golden globe of fruit
Or full-flushed flower peered out upon the road,
Nodding against the stone, and where he heard
Sometimes the voices of the chanting monks,
Sometimes the laugh of children at their play,
Amidst the quaint, old gardens. But these sights
Were in the suburbs of the wealthy towns.
For many a day through wildernesses rank,
Or marshy, feverous meadow-lands he fared,
The fierce sun smiting his close-muffled head;
Or 'midst the Alpine gorges faced the storm,
That drave adown the gullies melted snow
And clattering boulders from the mountain-tops.
At times, between the mountains and the sea

TANNHAÜSER.

Fair prospects opened, with the boundless stretch
Of restless, tideless waters by his side,
And their long wash upon the yellow sand.
Beneath this generous sky the country-folk
Could lead a freer life, — the fat, green fields
Offered rich pasturage, athwart the air
Rang tinkling cow-bells and the shepherds' pipes.
The knight met many a strolling troubadour,
Bearing his cithern, flute, or dulcimer;
And oft beneath some castle's balcony,
At night, he heard their mellow voices rise,
Blent with stringed instruments or tambourines,
Chanting some lay as natural as a bird's.
Then Nature stole with healthy influence
Into his thoughts; his love of beauty woke,
His Muse inspired dreams as in the past.
But after this came crueler remorse,
And he would tighten round his loins the rope,
And lie for hours beside some wayside cross,
And feel himself unworthy to enjoy
The splendid gift and privilege of life.
Then forth he hurried, spurred by his desire
To reach the City of the Seven Hills,
And gain his absolution. Some leagues more
Would bring him to the vast Campagna land,
When by a roadside well he paused to rest.
'Twas noon, and reapers in the field hard by

Lay 'neath the trees upon the sun-scorched grass.
But from their midst one came towards the well,
Not trudging like a man forespent with toil,
But frisking like a child in holiday,
With light, free steps. The pilgrim watched him come,
And found him scarcely older than a child,
A large-mouthed earthen pitcher in his hand,
And a guitar upon his shoulder slung.
A wide straw hat threw all his face in shade,
But doffing this, to catch whatever breeze
Might stir among the branches, he disclosed
A charming head of rippled, auburn hair,
A frank, fair face, as lovely as a girl's,
With great, soft eyes, as mild and grave as kine's.
Above his head he slipped the instrument,
And laid it with his hat upon the turf,
Lowered his pitcher down the well-head cool,
And drew it dripping upward, ere he saw
The watchful pilgrim, craving (as he thought)
The precious draught. "Your pardon, holy sir,
Drink first," he cried, "before I take the jar
Unto my father in the reaping-field."
Touched by the cordial kindness of the lad,
The pilgrim answered, — "Thanks, my thirst is quenched
From mine own palm." The stranger deftly poised

The brimming pitcher on his head, and turned
Back to the reaping-folk, while Tannhaüser
Looked after him across the sunny fields,
Clasping each hand about his waist to bear
The balanced pitcher; then, down glancing, found
The lad's guitar near by, and fell at once
To striking its tuned strings with wandering hands,
And pensive eyes filled full of tender dreams.
"Yea, holy sir, it is a worthless thing,
And yet I love it, for I make it speak."
The boy again stood by him, and dispelled
His train of fantasies half sweet, half sad.
"That was not in my thought," the knight replied.
"Its worth is more than rubies; whoso hath
The art to make this speak is raised thereby
Above all loneliness or grief or fear."
More to himself than to the lad he spake,
Who, understanding not, stood doubtfully
At loss for answer; but the knight went on:
"How came it in your hands, and who hath tuned
Your voice to follow it." "I am unskilled,
Good father, but my mother smote its strings
To music rare." Diverted from one theme,
Pleased with the winsome candor of the boy,
The knight encouraged him to confidence;
Then his own gift of minstrelsy revealed,
And told bright tales of his first wanderings,

When in lords' castles and kings' palaces
Men still made place for him, for in his land
The gift was rare and valued at its worth,
And brought great victory and sounding fame.
Thus, in retracing all his pleasant youth,
His suffering passed as though it had not been.
Wide-eyed and open-mouthed the boy gave ear,
His fair face flushing with the sudden thoughts
That went and came, — then, as the pilgrim ceased,
Drew breath and spake: " And where now is your
    lyre ? "
The knight with both hands hid his changed, white
    face,
Crying aloud, " Lost ! lost ! forever lost ! "
Then, gathering strength, he bared his face again
Unto the frightened, wondering boy, and rose
With hasty fear. " Ah, child, you bring me back
Unwitting to remembrance of my grief,
For which I donned eternal garb of woe;
And yet I owe you thanks for one sweet hour
Of healthy human intercourse and peace.
'Tis not for me to tarry by the way.
Farewell ! " The impetuous, remorseful boy,
Seeing sharp pain on that kind countenance,
Fell at his feet and cried, " Forgive my words,
Witless but innocent, and leave me not
Without a blessing." Moved unutterably,

The pilgrim kissed with trembling lips his head,
And muttered, "At this moment would to God
That I were worthy!" Then waved wasted hands
Over the youth in act of blessing him,
But faltered, "Cleanse me through his innocence,
O heavenly Father!" and with quickening steps
Hastened away upon the road to Rome.
The noon was past, the reapers drew broad swaths
With scythes sun-smitten 'midst the ripened crop.
Thin shadows of the afternoon slept soft
On the green meadows as the knight passed forth.

 He trudged amidst the sea of poisonous flowers
On the Campagna's undulating plain,
With Rome, the many-steepled, many-towered,
Before him, regnant on her throne of hills.
A thick blue cloud of haze o'erhung the town,
But the fast-sinking sun struck fiery light
From shining crosses, roofs, and flashing domes.
Across his path an arching bridge of stone
Was raised above a shrunken yellow stream,
Hurrying with the light on every wave
Towards the great town and outward to the sea.
Upon the bridge's crest he paused, and leaned
Against the barrier, throwing back his cowl,
And gazed upon the dull, unlovely flood
That was the Tiber. Quaggy banks lay bare,

Muddy and miry, glittering in the sun,
And myriad insects hovered o'er the reeds,
Whose lithe, moist tips by listless airs were stirred.
When the low sun had dropped behind the hills,
He found himself within the streets of Rome,
Walking as in a sleep, where naught seemed real.
The clattering hubbub of the market-place,
Was over now; but voices smote his ear
Of garrulous citizens who jostled past.
Loud cries, gay laughter, snatches of sweet song,
The tinkling fountains set in gardens cool
About the pillared palaces, and blent
With trickling of the conduits in the squares,
The noisy teams within the narrow streets, —
All these the stranger heard and did not hear,
While ringing bells pealed out above the town,
And calm gray twilight skies stretched over it.
Wide open stood the doors of every church,
And through the porches pressed a streaming throng.
Vague wonderment perplexed him, at the sight
Of broken columns raised to Jupiter
Beside the cross, immense cathedrals reared
Upon a dead faith's ruins; all the whirl
And eager bustle of the living town
Filling the storied streets, whose very stones
Were solemn monuments, and spake of death.
Although he wrestled with himself, the thought

Of that poor, past religion smote his heart
With a huge pity and deep sympathy,
Beyond the fervor which the Church inspired.
Where was the noble race who ruled the world,
Moulded of purest elements, and stuffed
With sternest virtues, every man a king,
Wearing the purple native in his heart?
These lounging beggars, stealthy monks and priests,
And womanish patricians filled their place.
Thus Tannhaüser, still half an infidel,
Pagan through mind and Christian through the
    heart,
Fared thoughtfully with wandering, aimless steps,
Till in the dying glimmer of the day
He raised his eyes and found himself alone
Amid the ruined arches, broken shafts,
And huge arena of the Coliseum.
He did not see it as it was, dim-lit
By something less than day and more than night,
With wan reflections of the rising moon
Rather divined than seen on ivied walls,
And crumbled battlements, and topless columns —
But by the light of all the ancient days,
Ringed with keen eager faces, living eyes,
Fixed on the circus with a savage joy,
Where brandished swords flashed white, and human
    blood

Streamed o'er the thirsty dust, and Death was
    king.
He started, shuddering, and drew breath to see
The foul pit choked with weeds and tumbled
    stones,
The cross raised midmost, and the peaceful moon
Shining o'er all; and fell upon his knees,
Restored to faith in one wise, loving God.
Day followed day, and still he bode in Rome,
Waiting his audience with the Cardinal,
And from the gates, on pretext frivolous,
Passed daily forth, — his Eminency slept, —
Again, his Eminency was fatigued
By tedious sessions of the Papal court,
And thus the patient pilgrim was referred
Unto a later hour. At last the page
Bore him a missive with Filippo's seal,
That in his name commended Tannhaüser
Unto the Pope. The worn, discouraged knight
Read the brief scroll, then sadly forth again,
Along the bosky alleys of the park,
Passed to the glare and noise of summer streets.
"Good God!" he muttered, "Thou hast ears for
    all,
And sendest help and comfort; yet these men,
Thy saintly ministers, must deck themselves
With arrogance, and from their large delight

In all the beauty of the beauteous earth,
And peace of indolent, untempted souls,
Deny the hungry outcast a bare word."
Yet even as he nourished bitter thoughts,
He felt a depth of clear serenity,
Unruffled in his heart beneath it all.
No outward object now had farther power
To wound him there, for brooding o'er those deeps
Of vast contrition was a boundless hope.

Yet not to leave a human chance untried,
He sought the absolution of the Pope.
In a great hall with airy galleries,
Thronged with high dignitaries of the Church,
He took his seat amidst the humblest friars.
Through open windows came sweet garden smells,
Bright morning light, and twittered song of birds.
Around the hall flashed gold and sunlit gems,
And splendid wealth of color, — white-stoled priests,
And scarlet cardinals, and bishops clad
In violet vestments, — while beneath the shade
Of the high gallery huddled dusky shapes,
With faded, travel-tattered, sombre smocks,
And shaven heads, and girdles of coarse hemp;
Some, pilgrims penitent like Tannhaüser,
Some, devotees to kiss the sacred feet.
The brassy blare of trumpets smote the air,

Shrill pipes and horns with swelling clamor came,
And through the doorway's wide-stretched tapestries
Passed the Pope's trumpeters and mace-bearers,
His vergers bearing slender silver wands,
Then mitred bishops, red-clad cardinals,
The stalwart Papal Guard with halberds raised,
And then, with white head crowned with gold in-gemmed,
The vicar of the lowly Galilean,
Holding his pastoral rod of smooth-hewn wood,
With censers swung before and peacock fans
Waved constantly by pages, either side.
Attended thus, they bore him to his throne,
And priests and laymen fell upon their knees.
Then, after pause of brief and silent prayer,
The pilgrims singly through the hall defiled,
To kiss the borders of the papal skirts,
Smiting their foreheads on the paven stone;
Some silent, abject, some accusing them
Of venial sins in accents of remorse,
Craving his grace, and passing pardoned forth.
Sir Tannhaüser came last, no need for him
To cry "Peccavi," and crook suppliant knees.
His gray head rather crushed than bowed, his face
Livid and wasted, his deep thoughtful eyes,
His tall gaunt form in those unseemly weeds,

Spake more than eloquence. His hollow voice
Brake silence, saying, "I am Tannhaüser.
For seven years I lived apart from men,
Within the Venusberg." A horror seized
The assembled folk; some turbulently rose;
Some clamored, "From the presence cast him
    forth!"
But the knight never ceased his steady gaze
Upon the Pope. At last, — "I have not spoken
To be condemned," he said, " by such as these.
Thou, spiritual Father, answer me.
Look thou upon me with the eyes of Christ.
Can I through expiation gain my shrift,
And work mine own redemption?" "Insolent
    man!"
Thundered the outraged Pope, "is this the tone
Wherewith thou dost parade thy loathsome sin?
Down on thy knees, and wallow on the earth!
Nay, rather go! there is no ray of hope,
No gleam, through cycles of eternity,
For the redemption of a soul like thine.
Yea, sooner shall my pastoral rod branch forth
In leaf and blossom, and green shoots of spring,
Than Christ will pardon thee." And as he spoke,
He struck the rod upon the floor with force
That gave it entrance 'twixt two loosened tiles,
So that it stood, fast-rooted and alone.

The knight saw naught, he only heard his judge
Ring forth his curses, and the court cry out
"Anathema!" and loud, and blent therewith,
Derisive laughter in the very hall,
And a wild voice that thrilled through flesh and
 heart:
"*Once being mine, thou art forever mine!*"
Half-mad he clasped both hands upon his brow,
Amidst the storm of voices, till they died,
And all was silence, save the reckless song
Of a young bird upon a twig without.
Then a defiant, ghastly face he raised,
And shrieked, "'Tis false! I am no longer thine!"
And through the windows open to the park,
Rushed forth, beyond the sight and sound of men.

By church nor palace paused he, till he passed
All squares and streets, and crossed the bridge of
 stone,
And stood alone amidst the broad expanse
Of the Campagna, twinkling in the heat.
He knelt upon a knoll of turf, and snapped
The cord that held the cross about his neck,
And far from him the leaden burden flung.
"O God! I thank Thee, that my faith in Thee
Subsists at last, through all discouragements.
Between us must no type nor symbol stand,

No mediator, were he more divine
Than the incarnate Christ. All forms, all priests,
I part aside, and hold communion free
Beneath the empty sky of noon, with naught
Between my nothingness and thy high heavens —
Spirit with spirit. O, have mercy, God!
Cleanse me from lust and bitterness and pride,
Have mercy in accordance with my faith."
Long time he lay upon the scorching grass,
With his face buried in the tangled weeds.
Ah! who can tell the struggles of his soul
Against its demons in that sacred hour,
The solitude, the anguish, the remorse?
When shadows long and thin lay on the ground,
Shivering with fever, helpless he arose,
But with a face divine, ineffable,
Such as we dream the face of Israel,
When the Lord's wrestling angel, at gray dawn,
Blessed him, and disappeared.
      Upon the marsh,
All night, he wandered, striving to emerge
From the wild, pathless plain, — now limitless
And colorless beneath the risen moon;
Outstretching like a sea, with landmarks none,
Save broken aqueducts and parapets,
And ruined columns glinting 'neath the moon.
His dress was dank and clinging with the dew;

A thousand insects fluttered o'er his head,
With buzz and drone; unseen cicadas chirped
Among the long, rank grass, and far and near
The fire-flies flickered through the summer air.
Vague thoughts and gleams prophetic filled his
  brain.
"Ah, fool!" he mused, "to look for help from
  men.
Had they the will to aid, they lack the power.
In mine own flesh and soul the sin had birth,
Through mine own anguish it must be atoned.
Our saviors are not saints and ministers,
But tear-strung women, children soft of heart,
Or fellow-sufferers, who, by some chance word,
Some glance of comfort, save us from despair.
These I have found, thank Heaven! to strengthen
  trust
In mine own kind, when all the world grew dark.
Make me not proud in spirit, O my God!
Yea, in thy sight I am one mass of sin,
One black and foul corruption, yet I know
My frailty is exceeded by thy love.
Neither is this the slender straw of hope,
Whereto I, drowning, cling, but firm belief,
That fills my inmost soul with vast content.
As surely as the hollow faiths of old
Shriveled to dust before one ray of Truth,

So will these modern temples pass away,
Piled upon rotten doctrines, baseless forms,
And man will look in his own breast for help,
Yea, search for comfort his own inward reins,
Revere himself, and find the God within.
Patience and patience!" Through the sleepless
    night
He held such thoughts; at times before his eyes
Flashed glimpses of the Church that was to be,
Sublimely simple in the light serene
Of future ages; then the vision changed
To the Pope's hall, thronged with high priests, who
    hurled
Their curses on him. Staggering, he awoke
Unto the truth, and found himself alone,
Beneath the awful stars. When dawn's first chill
Crept through the shivering grass and heavy leaves,
Giddy and overcome, he fell and slept
Upon the dripping weeds, nor dreamed nor stirred,
Until the wide plain basked in noon's broad light.
He dragged his weary frame some paces more,
Unto a solitary herdsman's hut,
Which, in the vagueness of the moonlit night,
Was touched with lines of beauty, till it grew
Fair as the ruined works of ancient art,
Now squat and hideous with its wattled roof,
Decaying timbers, and loose door wide oped,

Half-fallen from the hinge. A drowsy man,
Bearded and burnt, in shepherd habit lay,
Stretched on the floor, slow-munching, half asleep,
His frugal fare; for thus, at blaze of noon,
The shepherds sought a shelter from the sun,
Leaving their vigilant dogs beside their flock.
The knight craved drink and bread, and with respect
For pilgrim weeds, the Roman herdsman stirred
His lazy length, and shared with him his meal.
Refreshed and calm, Sir Tannhaüser passed forth,
Yearning with morbid fancy once again
To see the kind face of the minstrel boy
He met beside the well. At set of sun
He reached the place; the reaping-folk were gone,
The day's toil over, yet he took his seat.
A milking-girl, with laden buckets full,
Came slowly from the pasture, paused and drank.
From a near cottage ran a ragged boy,
And filled his wooden pail, and to his home
Returned across the fields. A herdsman came,
And drank and gave his dog to drink, and passed,
Greeting the holy man who sat there still,
Awaiting. But his feeble pulse beat high
When he descried at last a youthful form,
Crossing the field, a pitcher on his head,
Advancing towards the well. Yea, this was he,

The same grave eyes, and open, girlish face.
But he saw not, amidst the landscape brown,
The knight's brown figure, who, to win his ear,
Asked the lad's name. "My name is Salvator,
To serve you, sir," he carelessly replied,
With eyes and hands intent upon his jar,
Brimming and bubbling. Then he cast one glance
Upon his questioner, and left the well,
Crying with keen and sudden sympathy,
" Good Father, pardon me, I knew you not.
Ah! you have travelled overmuch : your feet
Are grimed with mud and wet, your face is changed,
Your hands are dry with fever." But the knight:
"Nay, as I look on thee, I think the Lord
Wills not that I should suffer any more."
"Then you have suffered much," sighed Salvator,
With wondering pity. " You must come with me;
My father knows of you, I told him all.
A knight and minstrel who cast by his lyre,
His health and fame, to give himself to God, —
Yours is a life indeed to be desired!
If you will lie with us this night, our home
Will verily be blessed." By kindness crushed,
Wandering in sense and words, the broken knight
Resisted naught, and let himself be led
To the boy's home. The outcast and accursed

Was welcomed now by kindly human hands ;
Once more his blighted spirit was revived
By contact with refreshing innocence.
There, when the morning broke upon the world,
The humble hosts no longer knew their guest.
His fleshly weeds of sin forever doffed,
Tannhaüser lay and smiled, for in the night
The angel came who brings eternal peace.

Far into Wartburg, through all Italy,
In every town the Pope sent messengers,
Riding in furious haste; among them, one
Who bore a branch of dry wood burst in bloom ;
The pastoral rod had borne green shoots of spring,
And leaf and blossom. God is merciful.

NOTE.

In spite of my unwillingness to imply any possible belief of mine that the preceding unrhymed narratives can enter into competition with the elaborate poems of the author of " The Earthly Paradise," yet the similarity of subjects, and the imputation of plagiarism already made in private circles, induce me to remark that " Admetus " was completed before the publication of the " Love of Alcestis," and " Tannhaüser " before the " Hill of Venus."

EMMA LAZARUS.

MISCELLANEOUS.

EPOCHS.

"The epochs of our life are not in the visible facts, but in the silent thought by the wayside as we walk." — EMERSON.

I. YOUTH.

SWEET empty sky of June without a stain,
    Faint, gray-blue dewy mists on far-off hills,
    Warm, yellow sunlight flooding mead and plain,
That each dark copse and hollow overfills;
The rippling laugh of unseen, rain-fed rills,
Weeds delicate-flowered, white and pink and gold,
A murmur and a singing manifold.

The gray, austere old earth renews her youth
    With dew-lines, sunshine, gossamer, and haze.
How still she lies and dreams, and veils the truth,
    While all is fresh as in the early days!
    What simple things be these the soul to raise
To bounding joy, and make young pulses beat,
With nameless pleasure finding life so sweet.

On such a golden morning forth there floats,
    Between the soft earth and the softer sky,
In the warm air adust with glistening motes,
    The mystic-winged and flickering butterfly,

A human soul, that hovers giddily
Among the gardens of earth's paradise,
Nor dreams of fairer fields or loftier skies.

II. REGRET.

Thin summer rain on grass and bush and hedge,
    Reddening the road and deepening the green
On wide, blurred lawn, and in close-tangled sedge;
    Veiling in gray the landscape stretched between
    These low broad meadows and the pale hills seen
But dimly on the far horizon's edge.

In these transparent-clouded, gentle skies,
    Wherethrough the moist beams of the soft June sun
Might any moment break, no sorrow lies,
    No note of grief in swollen brooks that run,
    No hint of woe in this subdued, calm tone
Of all the prospect unto dreamy eyes.

Only a tender, unnamed half-regret
    For the lost beauty of the gracious morn;
A yearning aspiration, fainter yet,
    For brighter suns in joyous days unborn,
    Now while brief showers ruffle grass and corn,
And all the earth lies shadowed, grave, and wet;

Space for the happy soul to pause again
   From pure content of all unbroken bliss,
To dream the future void of grief and pain,
   And muse upon the past, in reveries
   More sweet for knowledge that the present is
Not all complete, with mist and clouds and rain.

III. LONGING.

Look westward o'er the steaming rain-washed slopes,
   Now satisfied with sunshine, and behold
Those lustrous clouds, as glorious as our hopes,
   Softened with feathery fleece of downy gold,
   In all fantastic, huddled shapes uprolled,
Floating like dreams, and melting silently,
In the blue upper regions of pure sky.

The eye is filled with beauty, and the heart
   Rejoiced with sense of life and peace renewed;
And yet at such an hour as this, upstart
   Vague myriad longings, restless, unsubdued,
   And causeless tears from melancholy mood,
Strange discontent with earth's and nature's best,
Desires and yearnings that may find no rest.

IV. STORM.

Serene was morning with clear, winnowed air,
  But threatening soon the low, blue mass of cloud
Rose in the west, with mutterings faint and rare
  At first, but waxing frequent and more loud.
  Thick sultry mists the distant hill-tops shroud;
The sunshine dies; athwart black skies of lead
Flash noiselessly thin threads of lightning red.

Breathless the earth seems waiting some wild blow,
  Dreaded, but far too close to ward or shun.
Scared birds aloft fly aimless, and below
  Naught stirs in fields whence light and life are gone,
  Save floating leaves, with wisps of straw and down,
Upon the heavy air; 'neath blue-black skies,
Livid and yellow the green landscape lies.

And all the while the dreadful thunder breaks,
  Within the hollow circle of the hills,
With gathering might, that angry echoes wakes,
  And earth and heaven with unused clamor fills.
  O'erhead still flame those strange electric thrills.
A moment more, — behold! yon bolt struck home,
And over ruined fields the storm hath come!

V. SURPRISE.

When the stunned soul can first lift tired eyes
   On her changed world of ruin, waste, and wrack,
Ah, what a pang of aching sharp surprise
   Brings all sweet memories of the lost past back,
With wild self-pitying grief of one betrayed,
Duped in a land of dreams where Truth is dead!

Are these the heavens that she deemed were kind?
   Is this the world that yesterday was fair?
What painted images of folk half-blind
   Be these who pass her by, as vague as air?
What go they seeking? there is naught to find.
   Let them come nigh and hearken her despair.

A mocking lie is all she once believed,
   And where her heart throbbed, is a cold dead stone.
This is a doom she never preconceived,
   Yet now she cannot fancy it undone.
Part of herself, part of the whole hard scheme,
All else is but the shadow of a dream.

VI. GRIEF.

There is a hungry longing in the soul,
    A craving sense of emptiness and pain,
She may not satisfy nor yet control,
    For all the teeming world looks void and vain.
No compensation in eternal spheres,
She knows the loneliness of all her years.

There is no comfort looking forth nor back,
    The present gives the lie to all her past.
Will cruel time restore what she doth lack?
    Why was no shadow of this doom forecast?
Ah! she hath played with many a keen-edged thing;
Naught is too small and soft to turn and sting.

In the unnatural glory of the hour,
    Exalted over time, and death, and fate,
No earthly task appears beyond her power,
    No possible endurance seemeth great.
She knows her misery and her majesty,
And recks not if she be to live or die.

VII. ACCEPTANCE.

Yea, she hath looked Truth grimly face to face,
   And drained unto the lees the proffered cup.
This silence is not patience, nor the grace
   Of resignation, meekly offered up,
But mere acceptance fraught with keenest pain,
Seeing that all her struggles must be vain.

Her future clear and terrible outlies, —
   This burden to be borne through all her days,
This crown of thorns pressed down above her eyes,
   This weight of trouble she may never raise.
No reconcilement doth she ask nor wait;
Knowing such things are, she endures her fate.

No brave endeavor of the broken will
   To cling to such poor strays as will abide
(Although the waves be wild and angry still)
   After the lapsing of the swollen tide.
No fear of further loss, no hope of gain,
Naught but the apathy of weary pain.

VIII. LONELINESS.

All stupor of surprise hath passed away;
    She sees, with clearer vision than before,
A world far off of light and laughter gay,
    Herself alone and lonely evermore.
Folk come and go, and reach her in no wise,
Mere flitting phantoms to her heavy eyes.

All outward things, that once seemed part of her,
    Fall from her, like the leaves in autumn shed.
She feels as one embalmed in spice and myrrh,
    With the heart eaten out, a long time dead;
Unchanged without, the features and the form;
Within, devoured by the thin red worm.

By her own prowess she must stand or fall,
    This grief is to be conquered day by day.
Who could befriend her? who could make this small,
    Or her strength great? she meets it as she may.
A weary struggle and a constant pain,
She dreams not they may ever cease nor wane.

IX. SYMPATHY.

It comes not in such wise as she had deemed,
  Else might she still have clung to her despair.
More tender, grateful than she could have dreamed,
  Fond hands passed pitying over brows and hair,
And gentle words borne softly through the air,
Calming her weary sense and wildered mind,
By welcome, dear communion with her kind.

Ah! she forswore all words as empty lies;
  What speech could help, encourage, or repair?
Yet when she meets these grave, indulgent eyes,
  Fulfilled with pity, simplest words are fair,
  Caressing, meaningless, that do not dare
To compensate or mend, but merely soothe
With hopeful visions after bitter Truth.

One who through conquered trouble had grown wise,
  To read the grief unspoken, unexpressed,
The misery of the blank and heavy eyes, —
  Or through youth's infinite compassion guessed
  The heavy burden, — such a one brought rest,
And bade her lay aside her doubts and fears,
While the hard pain dissolved in blessed tears.

X. PATIENCE.

The passion of despair is quelled at last;
   The cruel sense of undeserved wrong,
The wild self-pity, these are also past;
   She knows not what may come, but she is strong;
She feels she hath not aught to lose nor gain,
Her patience is the essence of all pain.

As one who sits beside a lapsing stream,
   She sees the flow of changeless day by day,
Too sick and tired to think, too sad to dream,
   Nor cares how soon the waters slip away,
Nor where they lead; at the wise God's decree,
She will depart or bide indifferently.

There is a deeper pathos in the mild
   And settled sorrow of the quiet eyes,
Than in the tumults of the anguish wild,
   That made her curse all things beneath the skies;
No question, no reproaches, no complaint,
Hers is the holy calm of some meek saint.

XI. HOPE.

Her languid pulses thrill with sudden hope,
　That will not be forgot nor cast aside,
And life in statelier vistas seems to ope,
　Illimitably lofty, long, and wide.
What doth she know? She is subdued and mild,
Quiet and docile " as a weanéd child."

If grief came in such unimagined wise,
　How may joy dawn? In what undreamed-of
　　hour,
May the light break with splendor of surprise,
　Disclosing all the mercy and the power?
A baseless hope, yet vivid, keen, and bright,
As the wild lightning in the starless night.

She knows not whence it came, nor where it passed,
　But it revealed, in one brief flash of flame,
A heaven so high, a world so rich and vast,
　That, full of meek contrition and mute shame,
In patient silence hopefully withdrawn,
She bows her head, and bides the certain dawn.

XII. COMPENSATION.

'Tis not alone that black and yawning void
   That makes her heart ache with this hungry
      pain,
But the glad sense of life hath been destroyed,
   The lost delight may never come again.
Yet myriad serious blessings with grave grace
Arise on every side to fill their place.

For much abides in her so lonely life, —
   The dear companionship of her own kind,
Love where least looked for, quiet after strife,
   Whispers of promise upon every wind,
And quickened insight, in awakened eyes,
For the new meaning of the earth and skies.

The nameless charm about all things hath died,
   Subtle as aureole round a shadow's head,
Cast on the dewy grass at morning-tide;
   Yet though the glory and the joy be fled,
'Tis much her own endurance to have weighed,
And wrestled with God's angels, unafraid.

XIII. FAITH.

She feels outwearied, as though o'er her head
    A storm of mighty billows broke and passed.
Whose hand upheld her? Who her footsteps led
    To this green haven of sweet rest at last?
What strength was hers, unreckoned and unknown?
What love sustained when she was most alone?

Unutterably pathetic her desire,
    To reach, with groping arms outstretched in prayer,
Something to cling to, to uplift her higher
    From this low world of coward fear and care,
Above disaster, that her will may be
At one with God's, accepting his decree.

Though by no reasons she be justified,
    Yet strangely brave in Evil's very face,
She deems this want must needs be satisfied,
    Though here all slips from out her weak embrace.
And in blind ecstasy of perfect faith,
With her own dream her prayer she answereth.

XIV. WORK.

Yet life is not a vision nor a prayer,
   But stubborn work; she may not shun her task.
After the first compassion, none will spare
   Her portion and her work achieved, to ask.
She pleads for respite, — she will come ere long
When, resting by the roadside, she is strong.

Nay, for the hurrying throng of passers-by
   Will crush her with their onward-rolling stream.
Much must be done before the brief light die;
   She may not loiter, rapt in this vain dream.
With unused trembling hands, and faltering feet,
She staggers forth, her lot assigned to meet.

But when she fills her days with duties done,
   Strange vigor comes, she is restored to health.
New aims, new interests rise with each new sun,
   And life still holds for her unbounded wealth.
All that seemed hard and toilsome now proves small,
And naught may daunt her, — she hath strength for all.

XV. VICTORY.

How strange, in some brief interval of rest,
  Backward to look on her far-stretching past.
To see how much is conquered and repressed,
  How much is gained in victory at last!
The shadow is not lifted, — but her faith,
Strong from life's miracles, now turns toward death.

Though much be dark where once rare splendor shone,
  Yet the new light has touched high peaks unguessed
In her gold, mist-bathed dawn, and one by one
  New outlooks loom from many a mountain crest.
She breathes a loftier, purer atmosphere,
And life's entangled paths grow straight and clear.

Nor will Death prove an all-unwelcome guest;
  The struggle has been toilsome to this end.
Sleep will be sweet, and after labor rest,
  And all will be atoned with him to friend.
Much must be reconciled, much justified,
And yet she feels she will be satisfied.

XVI. PEACE.

The calm outgoing of a long, rich day,
    Checkered with storm and sunshine, gloom and
        light
Now passing in pure, cloudless skies away,
    Withdrawing into silence of blank night.
    Thick shadows settle on the landscape bright,
Like the weird cloud of death that falls apace
On the still features of the passive face.

Soothing and gentle as a mother's kiss,
    The touch that stopped the beating of the heart.
A look so blissfully serene as this,
    Not all the joy of living could impart.
    Patient to bide, yet willing to depart,
With dauntless faith and courage therewithal,
The Master found her ready at his call.

On such a golden evening forth there floats,
    Between the grave earth and the glowing sky
In the clear air, unvexed with hazy motes,
    The mystic-winged and flickering butterfly,
    A human soul, that drifts at liberty,
Ah! who can tell to what strange paradise,
To what undreamed-of fields and lofty skies!

February, 1871.

FLORENCE NIGHTINGALE.

Upon the whitewashed walls
    A woman's shadow falls,
A woman walketh o'er the darksome floors.
    A soft, angelic smile
    Lighteth her face the while,
In passing through the dismal corridors.

    And now and then there slips
    A word from out her lips,
More sweet and grateful to those listening ears
    Than the most plaintive tale
    Of the sad nightingale,
Whose name and tenderness this woman bears.

    Her presence in the room
    Of agony and gloom,
No fretful murmurs, no coarse words profane;
    For while she standeth there,
    All words are hushed save prayer;
She seems God's angel weeping o'er man's pain.

      And some of them arise,
      With eager, tearful eyes,
From off their couch to see her passing by.
      Some, e'en too weak for this,
      Can only stoop and kiss
Her shadow, and fall back content to die.

      No monument of stone
      Needs this heroic one, —
Her name is graven on each noble heart;
      And in all after years
      Her praise will be the tears
Which at that name from quivering lids will start.

      And those who live not now,
      To see the sainted brow,
And the angelic smile before it flits for aye,
      They in the future age
      Will kiss the storied page
Whereon the shadow of her life will lie.

March 7, 1867.

DREAMS.

A DREAM of lilies: all the blooming earth,
    A garden full of fairies and of flowers;
Its only music the glad cry of mirth,
    While the warm sun weaves golden-tissued hours;
Hope a bright angel, beautiful and true
    As Truth herself, and life a lovely toy,
Which ne'er will weary us, ne'er break, a new
    Eternal source of pleasure and of joy.

A dream of roses: vision of Love's tree,
    Of beauty and of madness, and as bright
As naught on earth save only dreams can be,
    Made fair and odorous with flower and light;
A dream that Love is strong to outlast Time,
    That hearts are stronger than forgetfulness,
The slippery sand than changeful waves that climb,
    The wind-blown foam than mighty waters' stress.

A dream of laurels: after much is gone,
    Much buried, much lamented, much forgot,
With what remains to do and what is done,
    With what yet is, and what, alas! is not,

DREAMS.

Man dreams a dream of laurel and of bays,
  A dream of crowns and guerdons and rewards,
Wherein sounds sweet the hollow voice of praise,
  And bright appears the wreath that it awards.

A dream of poppies, sad and true as Truth, —
  That all these dreams were dreams of vanity;
And full of bitter penitence and ruth,
  In his last dream, man deems 'twere good to die;
And weeping o'er the visions vain of yore,
  In the sad vigils he doth nightly keep,
He dreams it may be good to dream no more,
  And life has nothing like Death's dreamless sleep.

April 30, 1867.

ON A TUFT OF GRASS.

WEAK, slender blades of tender green,
With little fragrance, little sheen,
   What maketh ye so dear to all?
Nor bud, nor flower, nor fruit have ye,
So tiny, it can only be
   'Mongst fairies ye are counted tall.

No beauty is in this, — ah, yea,
E'en as I gaze on you to-day,
   Your hue and fragrance bear me back
Into the green, wide fields of old,
With clear, blue air, and manifold
   Bright buds and flowers in blossoming track.

All bent one way like flickering flame,
Each blade caught sunlight as it came,
   Then rising, saddened into shade;
A changeful, wavy, harmless sea,
Whose billows none could bitterly
   Reproach with wrecks that they had made.

ON A TUFT OF GRASS.

No gold ever was buried there
More rich, more precious, or more fair
   Than buttercups with yellow gloss.
No ships of mighty forest trees
E'er foundered in these guiltless seas
   Of grassy waves and tender moss.

Ah, no! ah, no! not guiltless still,
Green waves on meadow and on hill,
   Not wholly innocent are ye;
For what dead hopes and loves, what graves,
Lie underneath your placid waves,
   While breezes kiss them lovingly!

Calm sleepers with sealed eyes lie there;
They see not, neither feel nor care
   If over them the grass be green.
And some sleep here who ne'er knew rest,
Until the grass grew o'er their breast,
   And stilled the aching pain within.

Not all the sorrow man hath known,
Not all the evil he hath done,
   Have ever cast thereon a stain.
It groweth green and fresh and light,
As in the olden garden bright,
   Beneath the feet of Eve and Cain.

ON A TUFT OF GRASS.

It flutters, bows, and bends, and quivers,
And creeps through forests and by rivers,
  Each blade with dewy brightness wet,
So soft, so quiet, and so fair,
We almost dream of sleeping there,
  Without or sorrow or regret.

May 22, 1867.

IN THE JEWISH SYNAGOGUE AT NEWPORT.

HERE, where the noises of the busy town,
    The ocean's plunge and roar can enter not,
We stand and gaze around with tearful awe,
    And muse upon the consecrated spot.

No signs of life are here: the very prayers
    Inscribed around are in a language dead;
The light of the "perpetual lamp" is spent
    That an undying radiance was to shed.

What prayers were in this temple offered up,
    Wrung from sad hearts that knew no joy on earth,
By these lone exiles of a thousand years,
    From the fair sunrise land that gave them birth!

Now as we gaze, in this new world of light,
    Upon this relic of the days of old,
The present vanishes, and tropic bloom
    And Eastern towns and temples we behold.

Again we see the patriarch with his flocks,
    The purple seas, the hot blue sky o'erhead,

IN THE JEWISH SYNAGOGUE AT NEWPORT.

The slaves of Egypt, — omens, mysteries, —
  Dark fleeing hosts by flaming angels led.

A wondrous light upon a sky-kissed mount,
  A man who reads Jehovah's written law,
'Midst blinding glory and effulgence rare,
  Unto a people prone with reverent awe.

The pride of luxury's barbaric pomp,
  In the rich court of royal Solomon —
Alas! we wake: one scene alone remains, —
  The exiles by the streams of Babylon.

Our softened voices send us back again
  But mournful echoes through the empty hall;
Our footsteps have a strange unnatural sound,
  And with unwonted gentleness they fall.

The weary ones, the sad, the suffering,
  All found their comfort in the holy place,
And children's gladness and men's gratitude
  Took voice and mingled in the chant of praise.

The funeral and the marriage, now, alas!
  We know not which is sadder to recall;
For youth and happiness have followed age,
  And green grass lieth gently over all.

Nathless the sacred shrine is holy yet,
  With its lone floors where reverent feet once trod.
Take off your shoes as by the burning bush,
  Before the mystery of death and God.

July, 1867.

WINGS.

Dawn opes her pensive eyes,
  In the yet starry skies,
A roseate blush upon her cheek and brows.
  Her purple mantle still
  Lies on the sky-kissed hill,
And a blue, solemn shade thereon it throws.

  The earth lies hushed and calm,
  No chant of praise, no psalm
Riseth to greet the rose-crowned queen of day.
  Each blade of grass, each leaf,
  Stands out in sharp relief,
Against the rayless blue and silver gray.

  All nature seems to wait
  For some new deed of Fate;
The silence is a sacred, reverent prayer, —
  When hark! from some sweet throat
  One thrilling, quivering note
Fills with its tremulous music all the air.

  Then from the dewy grass
  A tiny form doth pass,

WINGS.

A little soul all music and all wings.
    All nature's voice is heard,
    Embodied in this bird,
That darteth up and, rising, ever sings.

    It mounteth still and sings :
    What soul yearns not for wings,
To follow after, burst its prison bars,
    And learn the secret there,
    In those clear realms of air, —
The secret of the rainbow and the stars ;

    To rush as swift as light,
    Within those regions bright
Of throbbing, scintillant, intensest blue ;
    The air all breathless cleave,
    And far below to leave
Regrets and tears, the raindrop and the dew.

    Ah! caged 'mongst meaner things,
    The soul can use no wings,
And beats against the bars it cannot pass ;
    But it might humbly turn,
    Essaying first to learn
The secret of the flowers and the grass.

November, 1867.

IN A SWEDISH GRAVEYARD.

"They all sleep with their heads to the westward. Each held a lighted taper in his hand when he died, and in his coffin were placed his little heart-treasures and a piece of money for his last journey."
LONGFELLOW, *Rural Life in Sweden.*

AFTER wearisome toil and much sorrow,
  How quietly sleep they at last,
Neither dreading and fearing the morrow,
  Nor vainly bemoaning the past!
Shall we give them our envy or pity?
  Shall we shun or yearn after such rest,
So calm near the turbulent city,
  With their heart stilled at length in their breast?

They all sleep with their heads lying westward,
  Where all suns and all days have gone down.
Do they long for the dawn, looking eastward?
  Do they dream of the strife and the crown?
Each one held a lit taper when dying:
  Where hath vanished the fugitive flame?
With his love, and his joy, and his sighing,
  Alas! and his youth and his name.

IN A SWEDISH GRAVEYARD.

The living stands o'er him and dreameth,
    And wonders what dreams came to him.
While the tender, brief twilight still gleameth,
    With a light strangely mournful and dim.
And he wonders what lights and what shadows
    Passed over these dead long ago,
When their feet now at rest trod these meadows,
    And their hearts throbbed to pleasure or woe.

What dreams came to them in their living?
    The self-same that come now to thee.
If thou findest those dreams are deceiving,
    Then these lives thou wilt know and wilt see:
The same visions of love and of glory,
    The same vain regret for the past;
All the same poor and pitiful story,
    Till the taper's extinguished at last.

All the treasures on earth that they cherished,
    Now they care not to clasp nor to save;
And the poor little lights, how they perished,
    Slowly dying alone in the grave!
With a flickering faint on the features
    Of age, or of youth in its bloom:
Lighting up for grim Death his weak creatures,
    In the darkness and night of the tomb,—

IN A SWEDISH GRAVEYARD.

With a radiance ghostly and mournful,
  On the good, on the just and unjust;
For a space, till the monarch, so scornful,
  Turned the light and the lighted to dust.
No taper of earth he desired
  In his halls where they quietly rest;
For all those who have toiled and are tired,
  Utter darkness and sleep may be best.

1867.

MARJORIE'S WOOING.

The corn was yellow upon the cliffs,
  The fluttering grass was green to see,
The waves were blue as the sky above,
  And the sun it was shining merrily.

"Marjorie, Marjorie! do you love me,
  Faithfully, truly as I love you?"
The little lass reddened, and whitened, and smiled,
  And answered him with her clear eyes of blue.

"Marjorie, you are but gentle and young;
  I am too old and too rough for you."
The little lass, trustfully giving her hand,
  Answered, "I love you, faithful and true."

"Marjorie, Marjorie, when shall we wed?"
  "As soon as you will it, — to-morrow, to-day."
"Marjorie, Marjorie, if you knew all,
  Would you still say me the words that you say?"

"If I knew all?" said the little lass,
  "I know you are Kenneth, the brave and strong;

MARJORIE'S WOOING.

I know that I love, and that you are good:
   I will know it e'er, and have known it long."

"Marjorie, Marjorie, if I should say
   I fled from prison to come to you;
I stabbed a man all for jealous love;
   I am not noble, nor good, nor true?"

"Kenneth, your eyes would belie your words,"
   Boldly and bravely the lass replied.
"Why should God fill them with love and truth,
   And your heart with cruelty, hate, and pride?"

"Marjorie, Marjorie, if I should say
   That I loved many ere I loved you?"
"Ere you had seen me," Marjorie said,
   "How could you know I was loving and true?"

"Marjorie, Marjorie, if I should say
   That I was outcast on land and on sea?"
"All the more reason," the little maid said,
   "Why you should ever be loved by me."

"Marjorie, Marjorie, if I should say
   That I was noble, and titled, and grand;
Lord of the woods, and the castle, and park,
   Lord of the acres of corn o'er the land?"

MARJORIE'S WOOING.

Dropping a courtesy, the little lass said,
    " Still should I love you and ever be true;
But if you found me too lowly and poor,
    I should bid farewell and go die for you."

" Marjorie, darling, I tell you then,
    This is the truth, and the land is mine,
And the castle, the park, and the vessel far off,
    And whatever is mine, is thine, dear, thine ! "

December 25, 1867.

THE GARDEN OF ADONIS.

(The Garden of Life in Spenser's " Faerie Queene.")

It is no fabled garden in the skies,
   But bloometh here, — this is no world of death;
And nothing that once liveth, ever dies,
And naught that breathes can ever cease to breathe,
   And naught that bloometh ever withereth.
The gods can ne'er take back their gifts from men,
They gave us life, — they cannot take again.

Who hath known Death, and who hath seen his face?
   On what high mountain have ye met with him?
Within what lowest valley is there trace
   Of his feared footsteps? in what forest dim,
In what great city, in what lonely ways?
Nay, there is no such god, but one called Change,
And all he does is beautiful and strange.

It is but Change that lays our darlings low,
   And, though we doubt and fear, forsakes them
     not.

Where red lips smiled do sweetest roses blow,
  And star-flowers bloom above the lovely spot
  Where gleamed the eyes, with blue forget-me-not.
And through the grasses runs the same wave there
We knew of old within the golden hair.

Dig in the earth, — ye shall not surely find
  Death or death's semblance; only roots of flowers,
And all fair, goodly things there live enshrined,
  With the foundations of the glad green bowers,
  Through which the sunshine comes in golden showers.
And all the blossoms that this earth enwreathe,
Are for assurance that there is no death.

O mother, raise thy tear-bathed lids again :
  Thy child died not, he only liveth more, —
His soul is in the sunshine and the rain,
  His life is in the waters and the shore,
  He is around thee all the wide world o'er;
The daisy thou hast plucked smiles back at thee,
Because it doth again its mother see.

What noble deed that ever lived, is dead,
  Or yet hath lost its power to inspire
Courage in hearts that sicken, and to shed
  New faith and hope when hands and footsteps tire,

THE GARDEN OF ADONIS. 173

And make sad, downcast eyes look upward higher?
Yea, all men see and know it, whence it came;
It purifies them like a burning flame.

And dreams? What dreams were ever lost and
    gone,
But wandering in strange lands we found again?
When least we think of these dear birdlings flown,
    We find that bright and fresh they still remain.
    The garden of all life is round us then;
And he is blind who doth not know and see,
And praise the gods for immortality.

May, 1868.

MORNING.

Gray-vested Dawn, with flameless, tranquil eye,
Cool hands, and dewy lips, is in the sky,
A sober nun, with starry rosary.

With eyes downcast and with uplifted palm,
She seems to whisper now her silent psalm;
Beneath her gaze the sleeping earth is calm.

Her prayer is ended, and she riseth slow,
And o'er the hills she quietly doth go,
Noiseless and gentle as the midnight snow.

Then suddenly the pale east blushes red,
The flowers to see upraise a sleepy head,
The rosy colors deepen, grow, and spread.

A cool breeze whispers: "She is coming now!"
And then the radiant colors burn and glow,
The white east blushes over cheek and brow,

And glorious on the hills the Morning stands,
Her saffron hair back-blown from rosy bands,
And light and joy and fragrance in her hands.

MORNING.

Her foot has touched the hill-tops, and they shine;
She comes, — the willow rustles and the pine;
She smiles upon the fields a smile divine,

And all the earth smiles back; from mount to vale,
From oak to shuddering grass, from glen to dale,
Wet fields and flowers and glistening brooks cry
  " Hail!"

IN MEMORIAM.

O FRIEND who passed away while flowers died,
   Now that the land bursts into bloom again,
With vivid blossoms o'er the landscape wide,
Purple and white 'mongst grasses golden-eyed,
   In beauteous resurrection o'er the plain, —

My thoughts revert to thee, who liest still,
   Under the pulsing, stirring, glowing earth;
Not rising with the lilac on the hill,
Not waking with the sunny daffodil,
   Living and breathing with no second birth.

In these sweet days I dream I see thy grave,
   A mockery of death, alive with flowers.
The delicate sprays and tender grasses wave,
Blue violets and the hardy crocus brave,
   Wooed back to life by sunshine, dew, and showers.

I cannot deem that thou art lying there,
   Asleep through all these fervent days of spring;
For I perceive thy spirit in the air,

Around me ever in my dream and prayer,
  Enskied and hallowed by thy suffering.

When thou didst walk upon the earth before,
  My trivial words and deeds alone were thine;
But now my holiest dreams are evermore
Blended with thoughts of thee, on that far shore,
  Where thy pale, girlish face has grown divine.

Through the dark shadows thou must go alone;
  And lo! thou hast a dauntless bravery,
A most majestic resignation shown;
A valiant patience, a faith not overthrown
  By the dread terror of uncertainty.

The day had fled, from thee for evermore,
  Thy soul was ebbing with the waning light,
And still thou asked, aweary and heartsore,
The same pathetic question o'er and o'er, —
  "O, I am tired! will I go to-night?"

Aye, thou didst go, — and where? Thou knowest
    now.
  Nature is innocent as well as fair;
Lilies, as well as amaranth, wreathe her brow.
She hath thy soul; because I cannot know
  Where it may be, I feel it everywhere.

178 IN MEMORIAM.

And thus the spring hath brought me flowers of
worth.
O mourners, cease to weep o'er empty graves!
Open them all! no dead come trooping forth,
To fill with ghastly hosts the living earth;
Only the flowers bloom, the green grass waves.

Those ye laid low with solemn rites and tears,
Elude you; while ye weep, they all have flown.
And so I lay aside my doubts and fears;
My friend in day-dreams and at night appears,
And hovers near when I am most alone.

REALITY.

"Hold fast to your most indefinite waking dream. Dreams are the solidest facts that we know." — HENRY D. THOREAU.

  CELESTIAL hopes and dreams,
And lofty purposes, and long rich days,
With fragrance filled of blameless deeds and ways,
  And visionary gleams, —

  These things alone endure ;
"They are the solid facts," that we may grasp,
Leading us on and upward if we clasp
  And hold them firm and sure.

  In a wise fable old,
A hero sought a god who could at will
Assume all figures, and the hero still
  Loosed not his steadfast hold,

  For image foul or fair,
For soft-eyed nymph, who wept with pain and
  shame,

For threatening fiend or loathsome beast or flame,
  For menace or for prayer.

  Until the god, outbraved,
Took his own shape divine; not wrathfully,
But wondering, to the hero gave reply,
  The knowledge that he craved.

  We seize the god in youth;
All forms conspire to make us loose our grasp, —
Ambition, folly, gain, — till we unclasp
  From the embrace of truth.

  We grow more wise, we say,
And work for worldly ends and mock our dream,
Alas! while all life's glory and its gleam,
  With that have fled away.

  If thereto we had clung
Through change and peril, fire and night and storm,
Till it assumed its proper, godlike form,
  We might at last have wrung

  An answer to our cries, —
A brave response to our most valiant hope.

REALITY.

Unto the light of day this word might ope
    A million mysteries.

O'er each man's brow I see
The bright star of his genius shining clear;
It seeks to guide him to a nobler sphere,
    Above earth's vanity.

Up to pure height of snow,
Its beckoning ray still leads him on and on;
To those who follow, lo, itself comes down
    And crowns at length their brow.

The nimbus still doth gleam
On these the heroes, sages of the earth,
The few who found, in life of any worth,
    Only their loftiest dream.

May, 1869.

HEROES.

In rich Virginian woods,
The scarlet creeper reddens over graves,
Among the solemn trees enlooped with vines;
Heroic spirits haunt the solitudes, —
The noble souls of half a million braves,
    Amid the murmurous pines.

Ah! who is left behind,
Earnest and eloquent, sincere and strong,
To consecrate their memories with words
Not all unmeet? with fitting dirge and song
To chant a requiem purer than the wind,
    And sweeter than the birds?

Here, though all seems at peace,
The placid, measureless sky serenely fair,
The laughter of the breeze among the leaves,
The bars of sunlight slanting through the trees,
The reckless wild-flowers blooming everywhere,
    The grasses' delicate sheaves, —

HEROES.

Nathless each breeze that blows,
Each tree that trembles to its leafy head
With nervous life, revives within our mind,
Tender as flowers of May, the thoughts of those
Who lie beneath the living beauty, dead, —
    Beneath the sunshine, blind.

For brave dead soldiers, these:
Blessings and tears of aching thankfulness,
Soft flowers for the graves in wreaths enwove,
The odorous lilac of dear memories,
The heroic blossoms of the wilderness,
    And the rich rose of love.

But who has sung their praise,
Not less illustrious, who are living yet?
Armies of heroes, satisfied to pass
Calmly, serenely from the whole world's gaze,
And cheerfully accept, without regret,
    Their old life as it was,

With all its petty pain,
Its irritating littleness and care;
They who have scaled the mountain, with content
Sublime, descend to live upon the plain;
Steadfast as though they breathed the mountain-air
    Still, whereso'er they went.

HEROES.

    They who were brave to act,
And rich enough their action to forget;
Who, having filled their day with chivalry,
Withdraw and keep their simpleness intact,
And all unconscious add more lustre yet
    Unto their victory.

    On the broad Western plains
Their patriarchal life they live anew;
Hunters as mighty as the men of old,
Or harvesting the plenteous, yellow grains,
Gathering ripe vintage of dusk bunches blue,
    Or working mines of gold;

    Or toiling in the town,
Armed against hindrance, weariness, defeat,
With dauntless purpose not to swerve or yield,
And calm, defiant strength, they struggle on,
As sturdy and as valiant in the street,
    As in the camp and field.

    And those condemned to live,
Maimed, helpless, lingering still through suffering
    years,
May they not envy now the restful sleep
Of the dear fellow-martyrs they survive?
Not o'er the dead, but over these, your tears,
    O brothers, ye may weep!

HEROES.

    New England fields I see,
The lovely, cultured landscape, waving grain,
Wide, haughty rivers, and pale, English skies.
And lo! a farmer ploughing busily,
Who lifts a swart face, looks upon the plain, —
    I see, in his frank eyes,

    The hero's soul appear.
Thus in the common fields and streets they stand;
The light that on the past and distant gleams,
They cast upon the present and the near,
With antique virtues from some mystic land,
    Of knightly deeds and dreams.

EXULTATION.

Behold, I walked abroad at early morning,
The fields of June were bathed in dew and lustre,
The hills were clad with light as with a garment.

The inexpressible auroral freshness,
The grave, immutable, aerial heavens,
The transient clouds above the quiet landscape,

The heavy odor of the passionate lilacs,
That hedged the road with sober-colored clusters,
All these o'ermastered me with subtle power,

And made my rural walk a royal progress,
Peopled my solitude with airy spirits,
Who hovered over me with joyous singing.

"Behold!" they sang, "the glory of the morning.
Through every vein does not the summer tingle,
With vague desire and flush of expectation?

"To think how fair is life! set round with grandeur;
The eloquent sea beneath the voiceless heavens,
The shifting shows of every bounteous season;

EXULTATION. 187

"Rich skies, fantastic clouds, and herby meadows,
Gray rivers, prairies spread with regal flowers,
Grasses and grains and herds of browsing cattle:

"Great cities filled with breathing men and women,
Of whom the basest have their aspirations,
High impulses of courage or affection.

"And on this brave earth still those finer spirits,
Heroic Valor, admirable Friendship,
And Love itself, a very god among you.

"All these for thee, and thou evoked from nothing,
Born from blank darkness to this blaze of beauty,
Where is thy faith, and where are thy thanksgivings?"

The world is his who can behold it rightly,
Who hears the harmonies of unseen angels
Above the senseless outcry of the hour.

SONNET.

STILL northward is the central mount of Maine,
   From whose high crown the rugged forests seem
   Like shaven lawns, and lakes with frequent gleam,
"Like broken mirrors," flash back light again.
Eastward the sea, with its majestic plain,
Endless, of radiant, restless blue, superb
With might and music, whether storms perturb
Its reckless waves, or halcyon winds that reign,
Make it serene as wisdom. Storied Spain
   Is the next coast, and yet we may not sigh
For lands beyond the inexorable main;
   Our noble scenes have yet no history.
   All subtler charms than those that feed the eye,
Our lives must give them; tis an aim austere,
But opes new vistas, and a pathway clear.

IDYL.

The swallows made twitter incessant,
   The thrushes were wild with their mirth.
The ways and the woods were made pleasant,
   And the flowering nooks of the earth.
And the sunshine sufficed to rejoice me,
   And the air was as bracing as wine,
And the sky and the shadows and grasses
   Were enough to make living divine.

Then I saw on the ground two gray robins,
   One with glorious flame-colored vest,
'Neath the shade of some delicate bluebells,
   By the breeze of the morning caressed.
They were singing of love in the shadow;
   She was bashful, and modest, and coy,
And he sang to her tenderest love-songs,
   And madrigals full of his joy.

And his song came forth clearer and clearer,
   With each passionate, musical note;
Like the ripple of silvery waters,
   It gushed from his beautiful throat.

His whole little bird-soul he offers, —
    Ah! she listens to him as he sings:
Then he ceases, awaiting her answer,
    With bright eyes and with quivering wings.

And I, too, stood awaiting it, breathless,
    For his song was too sweet to disdain,
Till it came, little notes full of gladness,
    With a plaintive and tender refrain.
And the songs died away in the distance,
    And the forest alone heard the rest,
As the two little lovers flew upward,
    To build them together a nest.

1868.

THE DAY OF DEAD SOLDIERS.

May 30, 1869.

WELCOME, thou gray and fragrant Sabbath-day,
  To deathless love and valor dedicate!
Glorious with the richest flowers of May,
  With early roses, lingering lilacs late,
With vivid green of grass and leaf and spray,
Thou bringest memories that far outweigh
  The season's joy with thoughts of death and fate.

What words may paint the picture on the air
  Of this broad land to-day from sea to sea?
The rolling prairies, purple valleys rare,
  And royal mountains, endless rivers free,
Filled full with phantoms flitting everywhere,
Pale ghosts of buried armies, slowly there
  From countless graves uprising silently.

A calm, grave day, — the sunlight does not shine,
  But thin, gray clouds bedrape the sky o'erhead.
The delicate air is filled with spirits fine,
  The temperate breezes whisper of the dead.

THE DAY OF DEAD SOLDIERS.

What visions and what memories divine,
O holy Sabbath flower-day, are thine,
   Painted in light against a field of red!

Behold the fairest spots in all the land,
   To-day in this mid-season of fresh flowers,
Are heroes' graves, — by many a tender hand
   Sprinkled with odorous, radiant-colored showers;
By mild, moist breezes delicately fanned,
Sending o'er distant towns their perfumes bland,
   Loading with sweet aroma sunless hours.

Who knows what tremulous, dusky hands set free,
   Deck quaintly with gay flowers the graves unknown?
What wealth of bloom is shed exuberantly,
   On the far grave in Illinois alone,
Where the last hero, sleeping peacefully,
Beyond detraction and mistrust, doth lie,
   By the glad winds of prairies overblown?

With hymns and prayer be this day sanctified,
   And consecrate to heroes' memories;
Not with wild, violent grief for those who died,
   O wives and mothers, but with patience wise,
Calm resignation, and a thankful pride,
That they have left their land a fame so wide,
   So rich a page of thrilling histories.

HOW LONG!

How long, and yet how long,
Our leaders will we hail from over seas,
Masters and kings from feudal monarchies,
    And mock their ancient song
With echoes weak of foreign melodies?

    That distant isle mist-wreathed,
Mantled in unimaginable green,
Too long hath been our mistress and our queen.
    Our fathers have bequeathed
Too deep a love for her our hearts within.

    She made the whole world ring
With the brave exploits of her children strong,
And with the matchless music of her song.
    Too late, too late we cling
To alien legends, and their strains prolong.

    This fresh young world I see,
With heroes, cities, legends of her own;
With a new race of men, and overblown
    By winds from sea to sea,
Decked with the majesty of every zone.

HOW LONG.

    I see the glittering tops
Of snow-peaked mounts, the wid'ning vale's expanse
Large prairies where free herds of horses prance,
    Exhaustless wealth of crops,
In vast, magnificent extravagance.

    These grand, exuberant plains,
These stately rivers, each with many a mouth,
The exquisite beauty of the soft-aired south,
    The boundless seas of grains,
Luxuriant forests' lush and splendid growth.

    The distant siren-song
Of the green island in the eastern sea,
Is not the lay for this new chivalry.
    It is not free and strong
To chant on prairies 'neath this brilliant sky.

    The echo faints and fails;
It suiteth not, upon this western plain,
Our voice or spirit; we should stir again
    The wilderness, and make the plain
Resound unto a yet unheard-of strain.

TRANSLATIONS.

FRAGMENT FROM THE ITALIAN OF GIACOMO LEOPARDI.

ANY a night I muse upon this shore:
And high above the varied plain I see
In the pure blue of heaven the flickering
    stars,
Glassed by the sea, and in the vault serene
They shine out scintillant around the world.
Steadfast I gaze upon those lights of heaven,
Which to mine eyes appear but points of flame,
And yet, in truth, are such stupendous worlds,
That unto them this earth is but a point.
Yea, unto them, not only man himself,
But all this great globe, whereon man is naught,
Is utterly unknown. And when I see
Clusters of stars, which unto us are film,
To which not only man, and this huge world,
But all these infinite orbs and golden suns
Are quite unknown, or else appear to them,
As they to us, a track of nebulous light,
Ah! then what seemest *thou* unto mine eyes,

O race of man? And when I call to mind
Thy state on earth, and then remember me
That thou dost deem thyself the lord of all,
And how thou dost presume to fable here
(On this dark grain of sand we call the earth)
Of the Creator of the universe;
When I recall the dreams that even now
Insult the wise, — what feelings and what thoughts
Rise in my heart, unhappy race of man!
Pity or scorn, I know not which prevails.

DEDICATION OF GOETHE'S "FAUST."

O HOVERING forms, ye come to me once more,
   Ye whom I saw in youth with troubled eyes.
Do I believe this dream as heretofore?
   Shall I essay to grasp it, ere it flies?
Ye crowd upon me, ye encompass me,
   As from the mist and vapor ye arise.
My bosom trembles at the breath again
Of the enchanted air about your train.

Ye bring to me the scenes of happy days,
   And many a lovely shadow reappears;
Like an old, half-forgotten tale, ye raise
   First-Love and Friendship of my early years.
Once more of all life's labyrinthine maze,
   The sad strain is repeated with fresh tears.
Ye name dear friends who have preceded me,
Cheated of lovely hours by Destiny.

The souls to whom I sang my early lay
   Hear not this last, — that friendly throng is gone,

The echo of the first has died away.
    Unto an alien public I intone
This my new song; their very plaudits make
My heart grow sick, and all who for my sake
In other days, on hearing me, made mirth,
If they still live, are scattered o'er the earth.

There seizes me a long unfelt desire
    For that calm spirit-region far away.
Above me floats, like an Æolian lyre,
    With indistinct, vague tones, my lisping lay.
I glow and tremble while tear follows tear,
And mild and soft becomes my heart severe.
All I have now seems strange and far to me,
And what hath gone becomes reality.

PROLOGUE FOR THE THEATRE.

(MANAGER. POET. MERRYMAN.)

MANAGER.

YE who so oft have stood by me in need
And trouble, say what hopes ye entertain
Of this our enterprise, on German ground.
I fain would please the public, — for they live
And let live, — now the posts are up, the boards
Are raised, and every one expects a feast.
They sit already, calm, with eyebrows arched,
And long to be amazed. I understand
How to propitiate the people's heart;
But I have ne'er before been thus perplexed.
True, they are not accustomed to the best,
But they are terribly well-read. And we,
How may we work, that all seem new and fresh,
And yet seem pleasing and instructive too?
I dearly love to see the multitude,
When towards our booth they throng, — a living
    stream, —
And press with powerful and constant waves

Unto the narrow entrance to our grace.
In the broad daylight, yea, ere four o'clock,
They thrust themselves towards the ticket-box,
And almost break their necks to buy a seat,
As I have seen them, in a year of dearth,
Crowd round the baker's shop for loaves of bread.
This miracle can only be performed,
On such a varied multitude, by one,
The Poet, — O perform it, friend, to-day.

POET.

Speak not to me of yonder motley throng,
  Whose very aspect bids the Muse take flight.
Hide from mine eyes that crowd whose billows
    strong
  Would drag us in the whirlpool with their might.
To some sweet, quiet corner lead my song,
  Where purest joy can bloom in heavenly light;
Where Love and Friendship can create and cherish,
With hands divine, delights that may not perish.

Ah! what hath sprung therein from out our soul,
  Or what the trembling, stammering lips let fall
(Now faltering, mayhap reaching now the goal),
  The power of the moment swallows all.
And often, after years successive roll,
In perfect shape it riseth to enthrall.

The glittering is for the hour we see,
The true abides for all posterity.

MERRYMAN.

Posterity! I ne'er would hear that name!
Were I to prate about posterity,
Who would make laughter for the present age?
For that they will, and that they ought to have.
The presence of a brave young lad, I think,
Is always something. He who understands
How to communicate his thoughts with grace,
Need never suffer from the public's whims.
His circle also must be very large,
That he may stir it with more certainty.
Be worthy thou, and make thyself a type;
Let Phantasy with all her followers,
Reason, Emotion, Sense, and Passion too
(Nor yet omit thou, Folly) find a voice.

MANAGER.

But more than all, find incident enough.
The world will come to look, and loves to see.
If much be spun before the public's eyes,
That they may gape with wonder and amaze,
Then you have gained in breadth immediately,
You are at once a popular young man.
The mass can only be subdued by mass.

Each one at last finds something for himself,
And every one goes home contentedly.
If you must give a piece, give it at once
In pieces; such a hash must needs succeed.
'Tis easily served, as easily as conceived.
What profits it to offer them a whole?
The public plucks it into pieces soon!

POET.

You cannot feel the baseness of such work.
  How little it becomes the artist true!
The hurried daubing of the finest spark
  Already is a maxim, then, with you.

MANAGER.

Such a reproof affects me in no wise.
Who works aright, must use the best of tools.
Consider this, — you have soft wood to split,
And only think for whom you are to write.
This one is driven here by tedium;
That one comes satiate from an o'erstocked board;
And worst of all, a goodly number come
Fresh from the daily papers. Here they haste,
With scattered wits as to a masquerade.
Mere curiosity wings every step.
The ladies give their presence and their dress,
And play for us without a salary.

What dream you on your heights of poetry?
What can amuse a crowded audience?
Look closely at the patrons of your art.
One half of them is cold, — one half is raw.
While one looks forward to a game of cards,
After the play, another one expects
A wild night on the bosom of some wench.
Wherefore, poor fools, to such an end as this,
Do ye torment the lofty Muse? I say,
Give more, and more, and ever more and more,
Then you can never fail to hit the mark.
Try only thou to mystify the world;
To satisfy is hard.
What have you gained?   Delight or pain?

POET.

           Away!
And seek thyself another slave, I say.
The poet, then, must cast by, wantonly,
The highest human privilege for thee;
The right of man that Nature has bestowed!
By what means has he found the royal road
To every heart? What arms to him are lent,
That he may vanquish every element?
What is it but the rare, harmonious strain
Within his breast, that sucks the world again,
Back to his heart? When Nature's listless hands

Spin the long thread that endlessly expands;
When the discordant crowd of beings clash,
Untuned and jarring, with a jangling crash,
Who re-creates them, and with gentle word,
Makes every circle move in sweet accord?
Who calls the individual to share
The universal, consecrating prayer,
With its celestial tones? Who maketh rage
The passions' storm, or can at once assuage,
And bid the rosy evening red abide
Within the mind serene? Who scatters wide,
Upon the loved one's path, fair buds of spring?
Or weaves the meaningless green leaves, to bring
A wreath that crowns the brow of genuine worth?
Who can ensure to dwellers on the earth,
Olympus, and with gods can meet and rest?
Man's power in the poet manifest!

MERRYMAN.

Employ these noble powers, and conduct
Your lyric business like a love affair.
You first approach by chance, — you feel, — you stay,
And get entangled by degrees. Joy grows, —
Anon it is disturbed; you are in bliss, —
Then enters Grief: and ere you are aware,
It is a romance. Be our play like this!

Grasp only in the thick of human life.
Each lives it, but 'tis known to very few,
And seize it where you will, it has a charm.
A little clearness among motley scenes,
Much error and a feeble spark of truth,
Thus is the liquor brewed that edifies
And quickens all the world. Youth's fairest flower
Assembles then to see your play, and hear
The revelation; then each tender mind
Imbibes therefrom its melancholy food.
Now one and now another is aroused,
And each sees what in his own heart he bears.
As yet they are prepared to laugh or cry;
They honor still the flight, and still rejoice
To see the sparkle. One completely formed,
Can ne'er be pleased; but one still being formed,
Is always grateful.

POET.

   Give me back the times
When I myself was being formed. My rhymes
Then gushed unbroken, fresh from their pure
  spring;
The world was veiled with mists, — a hidden thing.
The bud still promised wonders; I could cull
The thousand flowers whereof the vale was full.
 Then I had nothing, — yet enough, forsooth!
 Joy in delusion and the thirst for truth.

Give back those wild emotions of the boy,
The strength of hate, the deep and painful joy,
    The might of love. Give back to me my youth!

MERRYMAN.

Thou hast true need of youth, my worthy friend,
When foes press round thee in the bitter fight;
When lovely maids cling close around thy neck;
When the wreathed guerdon of the rapid course
Still beckons from the distant hard-won goal;
When, after the swift whirl of the mad dance,
You drink away the night in wassail wild.
But now, to strike the lyre with grace and strength
With sweet meanderings towards a self-made aim,
Must be your task, old gentleman; and we,
No less on that account, will honor you.
Age does not make us childish as they say,
It only find us all true children still.

MANAGER.

A truce to words and show us deeds at last;
While you exchange your compliments, the time
Goes by when something useful might be done.
Of what avail to talk of the fit mood?
It never comes to him who hesitates.
Declare yourself a poet openly,

And you command the Muse. You know our
    need;
We wish strong liquor, — brew away at once.
That which is not begun to-day, my friend,
To-morrow is not finished. Not one day
Is to be lost in idle dallying.
The firm man boldly grasps the possible,
Nor lets it slip, but works because he must.
You know each one upon our German stage
Can try whatso he please; so spare me not
Machinery nor scenic ornament.
Make use of heaven's great and lesser lights, —
Yea, you are free to squander e'en the stars.
We lack not water, rocks, beasts, birds, nor fire.
So traverse, in this narrow booth of ours,
The whole great circle of created things,
And journey on, with well-considered speed,
From highest heaven through the world to hell.

SCENE FROM "FAUST."

NIGHT. — *In a narrow, vaulted Gothic chamber, seated restlessly in his chair before his desk,* FAUST *is discovered.*

FAUST.

I have, alas! by zealous energy
Mastered philosophy and medicine,
With law, and, woe is me! theology;
Yet grow, poor fool, no wiser than before.
They call me Master, yea, and Doctor too;
For nine years I have led my pupils round,
By crooked ways and straight, and to and fro,
And see at last that nothing can be known.
This thought will break my heart! 'Tis true, indeed,
I am more clever than the solemn fools,
The doctors, authors, magistrates, and priests.
No doubts nor scruples vex me. I fear not
Hell nor the Devil; therefore joy is dead.
I dream no more my knowledge valuable, —
I dream no longer I can teach mankind
Aught to ennoble or to elevate.
Besides, I have not either money, lands,

Honor, nor rank : no dog would live like this !
So I devote myself to magic arts.
Perchance, through power of the soul and voice,
Many a mystery will be clear to me,
So that no longer I, with bitter sweat,
Must speak of what I do not understand;
So that I may discover what that is
That holds the world together at its heart,
See all the germs and forces of creation,
And drive no more a petty trade with words.

O that thou looked, full radiance of the moon,
For the last time upon my misery !
Thou for whose sake I waited at my desk
So many a midnight, till above my scrolls
And books, thou shone, my melancholy friend,
O that I might, upon the mountain-tops,
Roam in thy blessed light; with spirits flit
Above the mountain caves, and hover then
Over the meadow in thy misty light,
And there, disburdened of experience,
Make myself whole by bathing in thy dew.

Alas ! and am I in my prison yet,
Penned in this damp, accursed hole, where even
The precious light of heaven scarce can pierce
Mournfully through the painted window-panes;

Encompassed with worm-eaten, dusty heaps
Of books, piled upward to the vaulted roof,
Enwrapped with smoky paper; while around
Lie myriad boxes, glasses, instruments,
And ancient lumber? This, then, is thy world;
Thou callest this a world!
      Dost thou still ask
Why in thy breast thy heavy heart throbs loud,
And why an indefinable, vague fear
Smothers the aspirations of thy soul?
Thou art surrounded but by smoke and mould,
By wild beasts' skeletons and dead men's bones,
Instead of living nature, for which God
Created man.
    Away! away! escape
To the large fields! is this mysterious book
Of Nostradamus insufficient guide?
There thou wilt learn the orbits of the stars;
If Nature speaks, thy soul will apprehend,
As spirit talks with spirit. All in vain,
The dry thought here expounds the sacred sign.
O spirits, ye are hovering near me now;
Answer me, if ye hear me.

  [*He opens the book and gazes at the sign of the macrocosm.*

       Ah! what bliss
Thrills all my being at the very sight!

I feel the fresh, pure warmth of joyous life
Glow once again through all my nerves and veins.
Was it a god who traced this blessed sign,
That calms the tempest in my soul, that fills
My heart with joy, and by mysterious force
Reveals the powers of nature lying near?
Am I a god? all is so clear to me!
In these pure lines, I see before my soul
Nature at work. Ah! now I understand
For the first time the sage's apothegm:
"The world of spirits is not closed to thee,
But thine own sense is shut, thy heart is dead.
Up, scholar! rise and bathe thy earthly breast
Unwearied in the morning's rosy red."

                                           [*He contemplates the sign.*

Lo! how each weaves itself to form the whole!
One for the other only works and lives.
How heavenly forces rise and then descend,
And pass the golden buckets each to each,
With grace-diffusing wings from heaven to earth,
All making harmony throughout the All!

What a display! but only a display!
Where shall I seize thee, nature infinite?
O, where, ye breasts? ye sources of all life,
Whereon the heavens and the earth do hang,

Towards which the desolate soul aspires and yearns,
Ye gush, ye flow, and must I faint in vain?

    [*He closes reluctantly the book, and gazes upon the sign of the microcosm.*

How differently this sign affects my soul;
Thou, spirit of the earth, art nearer me.
Already do I feel my strength increased,
Already do I warm as with new wine.
Now I feel brave to meet the world, endure
The fullness of the grief and joy of earth;
To wrestle with the storm, and not to sink
'Midst all the crash of shipwreck.

                      Overhead,
The sky is clouded and the moon concealed,
The lamp-light flickers, noisome grows the air,
Red rays flash round my head, a tremor falls
From the high vault, and makes my flesh to creep.
I feel thee, thou art near me, spirit charmed
By prayer. Unveil! Alas, my heart is torn,
With strange emotions is my being thrilled;
I feel my whole soul given up to thee, —
Thou must! thou must! though it should cost my
    life!

    [*He seizes the book and repeats the incantation mystically. A rosy flame flashes up, and the spirit appears in the flame.*

SPIRIT.

Who calls me?

SCENE FROM "FAUST."

FAUST.

Awful apparition! Hence!

SPIRIT.

Thou hast compelled me with a mighty spell,
By sucking at my sphere — and now —

FAUST.

Away!

I cannot bear thee!

SPIRIT.

Thou hast long implored
Breathless to gaze upon me, hear my voice,
And see my countenance. Thy spells have worked
Upon my essence. I am here, and now
What miserable fear unmans thee thus?
Where is the invocation of thy soul?
Where is the breast that could create its world,
Cherish, uphold it, and with tremulous joy
Swell to uplift itself to equal height
With us the spirits? Where art thou, O Faust,
Whose voice rang through me, who aspired to me
With all thine energies? Art thou the same
Who shudder'st at my breath through all thy being,
A trembling, writhing worm?

SCENE FROM "FAUST."

FAUST.

       Creature of flame!
To thee shall I surrender? I am he,
Thine equal, Faust!

SPIRIT.

'Midst the tides of life, amidst action's storm,
Up and down I toss, to and fro I wave,
On infinite seas, 'twixt cradle and grave;
With various woof I spin bright life warm,
At Time's whirring shuttle eternally,
For the living apparel of Deity.

FAUST.

Ah, busy spirit, thou who compassest
The mighty world, how near I feel to thee!

SPIRIT.

Thou art that spirit's equal whom thy soul
Can understand, not mine!
         [*Vanishes.*

FAUST.

      Not thine! then whose?
I image of the Godhead, not even thine!
       [*A knock at the door.*
O death! I know it is my secretary,
My fairest fortunes he annihilates.

SCENE FROM "FAUST."

O that the dull, prosaic groveler
Should this profusion of bright dreams destroy!
    [*Enter* WAGNER *in his dressing-gown and night-cap, with a
    lamp in his hand. Faust turns to him with displeasure.*

WAGNER.

Pardon! I thought I heard your voice declaim;
Doubtless it was some Grecian tragedy.
Fain would I learn this art, for nowadays
It hath much influence; I oft have heard
That a good actor may instruct a priest.

FAUST.

Yea, if the priest be but an actor too,
As it may easily happen in these days.

WAGNER.

Ah! if one always must be thus confined
To study, and can only see the world
On holidays, as through a telescope,
Far, far remote, how can he lead it then
By his persuasion?

FAUST.

          If you feel it not,
You ne'er may hope to find by seeking it.
If it flows not from out your inmost soul,

With influences irresistible,
Subduing all the hearers' hearts, remain
Inactive ever; glue it, serve a hash
From others' feasts, and blow the petty flame
From out your little ash-heap with your breath,
Then you may gain applause from children, apes,
If you are able to endure such praise;
But your words ne'er will touch another's heart,
Unless they issue from the heart themselves.

WAGNER.

'Tis action makes the orator's success;
I feel it, but I may not yet attain.

FAUST.

Try honest means, and be no jingling fool.
Good sense and reason can express themselves
With little art. When you have aught to say
In earnest, have you then to hunt for words?
Yea, all the glittering eloquence wherewith
Men twist in shape the poorest shreds of thought,
Is unrefreshing as the misty wind,
That rustles through the autumn's withered leaves.

WAGNER.

Good Lord! but art is long, and life is short.
Oft in my critical pursuits, my head

And heart are both oppressed. How difficult
To gain the wherewithal to reach aright
The fountain-head! When we are but half-way,
Poor devils, we must die!

FAUST.

       Is parchment, then,
The holy well, whereof a single draught
Allays our thirst forever? You have gained
No cordial, if it gush not from your soul.

WAGNER.

Pardon, 'tis pleasant to transport one's self
Into the spirit of the times, — to see
How some wise man before us thought, and now
How gloriously far we have progressed.

FAUST.

O yea, up to the very stars! My friend,
The past is as a book with seven seals.
And what you call the spirit of the times,
At bottom is no more than your own soul,
Wherein the times are mirrored. Verily,
A pitiable sight, from which we flee,
At the first glance, — a dust-box, lumber-room,
At best a ceremonious puppet-show,
With excellent, pragmatic axioms,
Such as befit the mouths of puppets well.

WAGNER.

Ah! but the world, the heart and soul of man,
Fain would we all know something more of these.

FAUST.

What we call "knowing," — who dares name the
 child
By its right name? The few who aught have
 known,
Yet foolishly ne'er guarded their full hearts,
But showed the rabble all they felt and saw,
These have been ever crucified and burned.
Excuse me, friend, the night is far advanced;
We must break off at present our discourse.

WAGNER.

I still most willingly would keep awake,
To talk so learnedly. To-morrow morn
Will be the Easter; you will then permit
A few more questions. I have zealously
Pursued my studies, — much I know e'en now,
But I would fain know all.
[*Exit.*

FAUST (*alone*).

How Hope ne'er leaves entirely the brain,
That always clingeth to insipid trash,
And gropes for treasures with an eager hand,

And when it findeth earth-worms, is rejoiced!
Dare such a human voice sound in this place,
Where spirits have surrounded me? Alas!
I thank thee, ne'ertheless, most poor of all
The sons of men, who snatched me from despair,
That well-nigh had destroyed mine intellect.
Ah! so gigantic was the apparition,
That I could only feel myself a dwarf.

I, image of the Godhead, thought myself
Near to the mirror of eternal Truth,
Stripped of the earthly, 'midst the purity
And radiance of heaven, — whose free soul,
Above the cherubim, aspiring, strove
To flow through nature's veins, and to enjoy
The life of gods with their creative power.
For my presumption, how must I atone?
A thunder-word has swept me wide away.

I dare not now compare myself with you:
Albeit I had power to draw you here,
I had no power to hold you. In that hour,
I felt myself so little and so great,
You thrust me fiercely back upon the lot
Uncertain of humanity. And who
Will teach me now, and what must I avoid?
Must I obey that impulse? Ah, in sooth,

No less than our misfortunes, our own acts
Impede the progress of our lives.

To the sublime conceptions of the soul
A something strange and alien ever clings;
And when we have attained all worldly good,
We call the better, vanity and lies.
The glorious feelings that have given us life,
Grow torpid 'midst the turmoil of the world.

Though hopeful Fancy once, with daring flight,
Dilated to infinity, yet now
A narrow, humble space sufficeth her,
When fortune after fortune hath gone down,
Wrecked in Time's whirlpool. Care hath built her
    nest
In the heart's lowest depths, and hatches there
All secret sorrows, rocking ceaselessly,
Destroying all our pleasures and our peace.
She dons forever some new mask, — appears
Now as our house and land, our wife and child,
Now water, now as poison, sword, or fire.
We quake at all that never happeneth,
And what we never lose, we still deplore.
I am not like the gods, I feel it well,
But like the worm that burrows in the dust,
And, while it seeks its living in the earth,
Is crushed and buried 'neath the passer's foot.

SCENE FROM "FAUST."

Is not all dust that on a hundred shelves
Narrows for me these walls? this frippery,
With myriad forms of empty nothingness,
That limits me unto this world of moths?
Shall I find here the thing that I require?
And must I in a thousand volumes read
That men have everywhere been miserable,
That here and there hath been one happy soul?

What mean'st thou by that grin, thou hollow skull,
Save that thy brain, distracted like mine own,
Once groped for daylight in its zeal for Truth,
And went in twilight miserably astray?
O instruments, ye also gird at me,
With wheels and cylinders, with cogs and springs.
I waited at the door, — ye were the keys.
Your wards are twisted cunningly and well,
But ye will never raise the bolt. Alas!
In the broad light of day, inscrutable,
Will Nature not be robbed yet of her veil.
And what she opes not freely to the soul,
Thou canst not force with levers and with screws.
Thou, ancient lumber, though I use thee not,
Art here because my father needed thee.
Thou, scroll, hast been discolored by the smoke,
Since my dim lamp first flickered o'er my desk
'Twere better had I spent my little all,

Than here to toil, o'erburdened by that little.
Wouldst thou possess that which thy sires bequeathed,
Make use thereof, — for what we do not use,
Is a sore burden. What the hour creates,
That only can it profit by.
      But why
Are mine eyes fastened still upon that spot?
Has, then, that phial a magnetic power?
Why does all grow at once serenely bright,
As though the moonlight in the woods at night
Breathed suddenly around?
      All hail!
Thou precious phial, which I reverent grasp,
In thee I honor human wit and art.
Thou essence sweet of mild and sleepy drugs,
Strong extract of fine fatal juices, grant
Unto thy lord a token of thy grace.
I see thee, and mine anguish is assuaged;
I grasp thee, and the struggle doth abate.
The flood-tide of my spirit slowly ebbs.
Forms beckon to me from an ocean vast,
The glassy billows glitter at my feet.
Another day allures to other shores.
I see a chariot of flame descend,
As if on airy wings, — I am prepared,
Upon an unknown path, to dart through space,

SCENE FROM "FAUST."

Towards other spheres of pure activity.
This lofty life, this godlike ecstasy,
Hast thou deserved it, thou erewhile a worm?
Yea, only resolutely turn thy back
Upon the lovely sun of earth, — be firm
To rend the gates asunder, which all men
Would willingly steal past. The hour hath come
To prove by action that man's dignity
Yields not to God's sublimity. Fear not,
At that dark hell where Fancy damns herself
To her own tortures, — struggle ever on,
Unto that pass around whose narrow mouth
All hell is flaming. Resolutely act,
Though at the peril of annihilation!

Then come to me, O pure and crystal cup,
Whereon I have not thought for many years,
From out your old receptacle. You shone
At merry-makings of my fathers, warmed
The serious guests who pledged you each to each.
It was the drinker's task to illustrate
By rhyme the rich and cunning images
Upon you painted, and with one long draught
To drain your contents. At the sight of thee,
I can recall how many youthful nights!
Now I will pass thee to no neighbor guest,
I will not test my wit upon thine art.

SCENE FROM "FAUST."

Here is a juice that soon intoxicàtes,
And with its dark brown liquor fills thy bowl.
Let this last draught, which I have here prepared
And chosen, now be quaffed with all my soul,
A sacred, festal greeting to the morn!
> [*He raises the goblet to his lips. Ringing of bells, and singing of choruses.*

CHORUS OF ANGELS.

Lo, Jesus hath arisen!
  Joy in His resurrection,
  O men, whom imperfection,
  Deceitful and pernicious,
  Hereditary, vicious,
Doth limit and imprison!

FAUST.

What mellow music, what deep humming draws
The goblet from my mouth? O hollow bells,
Are ye announcing now the festal hour
Of Easter morn? Already, O ye choirs,
Do ye begin the sweet, consoling hymn,
That once, amid the darkness of the grave,
Rang forth from angels' lips, — assurance glad
Of a new covenant?

SCENE FROM "FAUST."

CHORUS OF WOMEN.

With myrrh and spicery
We have embalmed Him, — we,
The faithful, laid Him out.
We swathed him round about,
His cerements did wind
   Cleanly upon His bier.
Alas! and now we find
   Christ no longer here.

CHORUS OF ANGELS.

Christ from the grave hath soared.
   The loving One is blest,
   Who stood the chastening test,
   In sad affliction bore
   The wholesome trial sore,
And suffered for his Lord!

FAUST.

Wherefore, O soft yet strong celestial tones,
Have ye thus sought and found me in the dust?
Resound ye rather where weak men abide.
I hear the message, but I lack the faith.
The favorite child of Faith is Miracle.
Unto those spheres, whence these sweet tidings
   sound,
I dare not e'en aspire; yet from my youth,

Familiar with this strain, it even now
Recalleth me to life. In former days
I felt the very kiss of heavenly love,
In the still Sabbath's solemn quietude.
The full tones of the bell resounded then
With such a depth of meaning, and a prayer
Was ardent happiness! Through wood and field
A yearning unimaginably sweet
Impelled me, — 'midst a thousand burning tears
I saw a world arise. This hymn announced
The sports of youth, the all-unfettered bliss
Of the spring festivals. Now memory
Restrains me with a child-like feeling still,
From the last solemn step. Ring forth again,
Ye sweet and heavenly refrains, — ring forth!
The tear is flowing, earth hath won me back!

CHORUS OF YOUNG MEN.

The Buried One has soared
   Already to the skies,
Our living, supreme Lord
   In glory doth arise.
His joy in resurrection,
   Is equal and akin
To God's joy in creating.
   We suffer still and sin.

He left us here, the faithful,
  His glad return to wait,
Alas! we are lamenting,
  Master, Thy happy fate!

      CHORUS OF ANGELS.

From mortality's womb,
  Lo, Christ hath arisen!
As He from the tomb,
  Escape ye from prison.
Ye bowing before Him,
Who by actions adore Him,
With joyful thanksgiving,
In brotherhood living,
Who promise and preach of Him,
The ignorant teach of Him,
For you is the Master here,
  You is He near!

SONG FROM HEINE.

My heart, my heart is heavy,
  Though merrily blooms the May;
Out on the ancient bastion,
  Under the lindens I stay.

There stands by yon gray old tower,
  The sentry-house of the town;
A red clad peasant soldier
  Goes pacing up and down.

He toys with his shining musket,
  That gleams in the sunset red,
Presenting and shouldering arms now, —
  I wish he would shoot me dead!

THE END